SCHOOLING, EXPERIENCE, AND EARNINGS

NATIONAL BUREAU OF ECONOMIC RESEARCH
Human Behavior and Social Institutions

SCHOOLING, EXPERIENCE, AND EARNINGS 1974

JACOB MINCER
National Bureau of Economic Research
and Columbia University

NATIONAL BUREAU OF ECONOMIC RESEARCH
New York   1974
Distributed by COLUMBIA UNIVERSITY PRESS
New York and London

HC
110.15
M55

235431

Relation of the Directors to the Work and Publications of the National Bureau of Economic Research

1. The object of the National Bureau of Economic Research is to ascertain and to present to the public important economic facts and their interpretation in a scientific and impartial manner. The Board of Directors is charged with the responsibility of ensuring that the work of the National Bureau is carried on in strict conformity with this object.

2. The President of the National Bureau shall submit to the Board of Directors, or to its Executive Committee, for their formal adoption all specific proposals for research to be instituted.

3. No research report shall be published until the President shall have submitted to each member of the Board the manuscript proposed for publication, and such information as will, in his opinion and in the opinion of the author, serve to determine the suitability of the report for publication in accordance with the principles of the National Bureau. Each manuscript shall contain a summary drawing attention to the nature and treatment of the problem studied, the character of the data and their utilization in the report, and the main conclusions reached.

4. For each manuscript so submitted, a special committee of the Directors (including Directors Emeriti) shall be appointed by majority agreement of the President and Vice Presidents (or by the Executive Committee in case of inability to decide on the part of the President and Vice Presidents), consisting of three Directors selected as nearly as may be one from each general division of the Board. The names of the special manuscript committee shall be stated to each Director when the manuscript is submitted to him. It shall be the duty of each member of the special manuscript committee to read the manuscript. If each member of the manuscript committee signifies his approval within thirty days of the transmittal of the manuscript, the report may be published. If at the end of that period any member of the manuscript committee withholds his approval, the President shall then notify each member of the Board, requesting approval or disapproval of publication, and thirty days additional shall be granted for this purpose. The manuscript shall then not be published unless at least a majority of the entire Board who shall have voted on the proposal within the time fixed for the receipt of votes shall have approved.

5. No manuscript may be published, though approved by each member of the special manuscript committee, until forty-five days have elapsed from the transmittal of the report in manuscript form. The interval is allowed for the receipt of any memorandum of dissent or reservation, together with a brief statement of his reasons, that any member may wish to express; and such memorandum of dissent or reservation shall be published with the manuscript if he so desires. Publication does not, however, imply that each member of the Board has read the manuscript, or that either members of the Board in general or the special committee have passed on its validity in every detail.

6. Publications of the National Bureau issued for informational purposes concerning the work of the Bureau and its staff, or issued to inform the public of activities of Bureau staff, and volumes issued as a result of various conferences involving the National Bureau shall contain a specific disclaimer noting that such publication has not passed through the normal review procedures required in this resolution. The Executive Committee of the Board is charged with review of all such publications from time to time to ensure that they do not take on the character of formal research reports of the National Bureau, requiring formal Board approval.

7. Unless otherwise determined by the Board or exempted by the terms of paragraph 6, a copy of this resolution shall be printed in each National Bureau publication.

*(Resolution adopted October 25, 1926, and revised February 6, 1933,
February 24, 1941, April 20, 1968, and September 17, 1973)*

Contents

Tables

Figures

Charts
(all charts are for white, nonfarm men)

Acknowledgments

This study is a direct descendant of my doctoral dissertation "A Study of Personal Income Distribution," Columbia University, 1957. A short version of the thesis appeared as "Investment in Human Capital and Personal Income Distribution" in the *Journal of Political Economy*, August 1958. Since that time, the economic analysis of human capital has grown into a large and vital field. The present study is in part a replication, on the much richer 1960 Census data (1/1,000 sample), of the research on the 1950 data reported in my thesis. More importantly, it represents a feedback into the field of income distribution of developments in human capital analysis which have occupied my attention since 1957. Throughout this time I was privileged to work closely with Gary S. Becker whose thinking gave form and direction to an entire field of economic analysis. I gratefully credit much of the conceptual advance of the present study over the 1957 vintage to this collaboration.

Other friends and co-workers who helped to convert the first draft into the present manuscript were Orley Ashenfelter, Yoram Ben-Porath, Barry R. Chiswick, John C. Hause, Robert T. Michael, Carl Rahm, Sherwin Rosen, Theodore Schultz, and Finis R. Welch.

I owe special thanks to my students in labor economics at Columbia University. Though a captive audience, they have been both receptive to and critical of the materials first tried on them and eventually incorporated here.

I was particularly fortunate to have the competent and devoted research assistance of Masanori Hashimoto, Sara Paroush, and Odile Cornet.

Research here reported was initially funded by the Economic Development Administration of the U.S. Department of Commerce, and later by the Office of Economic Opportunity and the National Science Foundation. This support is gratefully acknowledged. Of course, the opinions expressed here are my own, and should not be construed as representing the opinions or policy of these agencies.

The book was edited and prepared for press by Ester Moskowitz, and the charts were drawn by H. Irving Forman.

Foreword

In 1957 Jacob Mincer completed his thesis, "A Study of Personal Income Distribution," one of the pioneering works in the new and illuminating literature on investment in human capital. He directed our attention to the importance of training, both in school and on-the-job, as a major explanation of income inequality.[1] Since then Mincer has enriched our understanding of economic behavior with seminal studies of labor force participation, consumption, and opportunity costs. Unresolved problems concerning income distribution were never far from his mind, however, and in recent years he has attacked them with renewed vigor. The result is this volume, surely one of the most important ever published on this subject and the most systematic one relying on the human capital approach.

In the pages that follow Mincer demonstrates his skill as a wielder of Occam's razor. His objective is to explain a great deal with a little. The subject is earnings inequality, but the reader will look in vain for references to unions, monopsonists, minimum wage laws, discrimination, luck, and the numerous other institutional factors that are frequently introduced in such studies. Instead, Mincer fashions a simple but powerful theoretical model in which human capital is the central explanatory variable. Mincer does not deny that other factors may influence earnings. His position is, "Let's see how far the human capital model can take us." And in his hands it takes us very far indeed.

The two principal elements of human capital in the model are schooling and post-school investment. In the absence of specific measures of post-school investment, Mincer uses experience, which he estimates from age and the length of schooling. In the theoretical section Mincer shows in convincing fashion that it is years of experience rather than age that should be emphasized in attempts to

---

1. See Jacob Mincer, "Investment in Human Capital and Personal Income Distribution," *Journal of Political Economy,* August 1958.

explain variations in earnings. If one simply holds age fixed, estimates of the return to schooling are biased downward because at a given age those with less schooling have more experience, having left school earlier.

In highly simplified form, the story Mincer unfolds is the following: If you choose at random a group of white nonfarm men of various ages and educational attainments, the differences in their education will explain only a small part (about 7 per cent) of the difference in their earnings. This is also what other researchers have found; unfortunately some have rushed to the conclusion that the remaining difference must be the result of "luck" or "personality." [2] Mincer notes that men who have the same amount of schooling may have very different amounts of labor force experience, and that they also will probably differ in the amount of post-schooling investment that they have. Those who engage in a great deal of post-school investment (extreme examples would be medical residents or law clerks) will have their earnings depressed (below what they could have earned) during the early portion of their working life. In later years, however, their earnings will be inflated by the return on that investment.

The best time to measure the effect of schooling on the earnings of a cohort of men is about eight years after they leave school. At this point of "overtaking," there is minimum distortion from post-school investment because their return on previous investment is just about equal to the cost of current investment. Mincer finds that at this point differences in schooling explain about *one-third* of the inequality in annual earnings. When account is taken of differences in weeks worked the explanatory power goes to over 50 per cent! Mincer points out that if the quality of schooling could be controlled,[3] the explanatory power of the human capital model would be increased further.

Mincer shows empirically that schooling has more explanatory power for groups with constant years of experience than for groups of the same age, and that the explanatory power is at its peak for groups with seven to nine years of experience. This result is pre-

---

2. See Christopher Jencks et al., *Inequality* (New York: Basic Books, 1972).

3. See Lewis Solmon, "The Definition and Impact of College Quality," Working Paper 7 (New York: NBER, 1973).

dicted in the theoretical section. By contrast the "credentials" argument of the effect of schooling does not yield such a prediction.

Mincer's insistence that experience matters more than age finds strong confirmation in the data on female earnings — mentioned only briefly in this volume. The age-earnings profile for married women, whose work experience is often interrupted, is much flatter than that of never-married women, who typically have at any given age a much more continuous attachment to the labor force and longer work experience.[4]

When Mincer began his research, public interest in problems of income distribution was minimal. Economic growth was the vogue, and rapid growth was supposed to make life so much better for everyone that relative shares would be of minor consequence. Not so today. A quarter century of rapid growth (real GNP per capita in 1973 is almost double what it was in 1948) finds us more concerned than ever about poverty and inequality.

Strong policy debates rage over whether and how the distribution of income should be changed. In keeping with NBER policy, this volume takes no side in this debate, offers no policy recommendations. Instead, Mincer provides a logical, coherent, albeit incomplete explanation of why the distribution of earnings is what it is — surely an invaluable contribution for anyone who wants to decide if or how to change the distribution.

I have stressed the book's positive contributions to economic science; the inevitable qualifications and caveats that should accompany such an ambitious work are amply provided by Mincer himself. Indeed his own characterization of it as "an early and quite rudimentary effort toward a systematic analysis of personal income distribution," offers the promise that we can look forward to further instalments in this lifetime of scholarship.

VICTOR R. FUCHS
*Vice President-Research; Director, Center for
Economic Analysis of Human Behavior and Social Institutions*

---

4. See Victor R. Fuchs, "Differences in Hourly Earnings Between Men and Women," *Monthly Labor Review,* May 1971; and Jacob Mincer and Solomon Polachek, "Family Investments in Human Capital: Earnings of Women," *Journal of Political Economy,* March 1974.

SCHOOLING, EXPERIENCE, AND EARNINGS

Introduction

The positive relation between an individual's schooling and his subsequent earnings may be understood to reflect productivity-augmenting effects of education. This relation is by no means direct or simple. Schooling and education are not synonymous: the educational content of time spent at school ranges from superb to miserable. The absorption of learning and marketability of knowledge and of skills acquired through learning also differ a great deal among individuals, places, and times. Moreover, school is neither the only nor necessarily the most important training ground for shaping market productivities. Finally, nonpecuniary aspects of work, temporary and long-run deviations from equilibrium wage rates and differences in the amount of time spent in employment in the labor market create additional differences among individual earnings, particularly when these are observed over a relatively short period.

It is not surprising, therefore, that observed correlations between educational attainment, measured in years spent at school, and earnings of individuals, although positive are relatively weak. Still, when earnings are averaged over groups of individuals differing in schooling, clear and strong differentials emerge. The initial and simplest form of the human capital model elaborated in this study[1] is addressed to these schooling group differentials in earnings. The scope of the model is then enlarged to deal with earnings differentials among age groups within the various schooling groups. This is accomplished by relating earnings to training on the job and to other human capital investments that follow the schooling stage of the life cycle.[2] Finally, by admitting into the model individual variations

---

1. As expressed in equation (1.1), this model was presented in Mincer (1957 and 1958).

2. The conceptual framework for this part of the analysis originates in Becker's *Human Capital* (1964). Its empirical application to observed age-income profiles is shown in Mincer (1962b). The approach here is similar, though the focus is reversed.

in investments and productivity within schooling groups and after completion of schooling, some insights are obtained about the distribution of earnings *within* age-education groups and in the aggregate.

The basic objective of this study is to gain some understanding of the observed distributions and structures of earnings from information on the distribution of accumulated net investments in human capital among workers. The basic operational concept is the human capital earnings function, by which the two distributions—of earnings and of net investment in human capital—are related. The earnings function is fashioned in the theoretical analysis in Part I. It is the major tool of the empirical analysis in Part II. An individual's "earnings profile" reflects his lifetime acquisition of human capital, and the aggregate distribution of earnings is viewed simply as a distribution of individual earnings profiles.

Clearly, this work is an early and quite rudimentary attempt at a systematic analysis of personal income distribution. Rapidly progressing research in human capital and in various aspects of income distribution suggests that the foundations that emerge in this and related studies will be consolidated and built upon. The major limitation, at the present time, is the absence of adequate information on individual investments in human capital. The accumulations of net investments that can be ascribed to individuals do not add up to their total capital stock because "initial" capacities and investments provided in and by the home environment are excluded. Still, the inclusion in the earnings function of even crude measures of "post-school investments" in addition to schooling lends a great deal of scope to the analysis of income distribution.

Individuals differ not only in the quantities of their accumulated investments but also in the rates of return they receive. We have no individual information on such rates. Variation in rates of return is probably an important aspect of the distribution of earnings. I treat it as part of the residual variation in the analysis, which relates earnings to volumes of investment. Much of the residual variation, however, is due to unmeasured quantities of human capital. It is not legitimate, therefore, to describe residual variation as a variation in rates of return, and even less so as a measure of risk in human capital investment. The same ambiguity applies to one of the sources of variation in rates of return, namely, to ability: it is not clear to what extent, if at all, various "ability" measures represent unobserved components of the human capital stock, or genuine efficiency parameters.

Other limitations of the study are self-imposed. These are spelled out in the appropriate context, and discussed as subjects for future research (see Chapter 8). The working model in the present study is stripped to bare essentials: the surprising scope of its empirical power is the major conclusion and promise to be drawn from it for further development.

Use of the human capital approach does not imply that alternative models of earnings distributions are invalid.[3] In many respects, the various approaches are complementary rather than mutually exclusive. At any rate, the emphasis of the present study is not on the testing of competing hypotheses, though some attention is paid to that, but on a coherent interpretation of detailed empirical characteristics of earnings distributions. The usefulness of the human capital approach lies in the extent to which such a unified interpretation is possible.

The following is a brief guide through the contents of the study:

Part I is a theoretical analysis of the relation between human capital accumulation and earnings. In Chapter 1, this relation is analyzed at the individual level, leading to a formulation of the individual earnings profile. In Chapter 2, the analysis is extended to a cross section of individuals. The cross-sectional distribution of earnings is viewed as a distribution of earnings profiles of individuals who differ in accumulations of human capital acquired at school and in post-school work experience.

Part II is an empirical analysis of earnings of white, urban, non-student men [4] observed in the 1/1,000 sample of the 1960 U.S. Census. Chapter 3 is an application of the "schooling model," in which human capital investments are restricted to schooling. This model is shown to be misleading, unless it is applied to a particular subset of workers, namely, those with somewhat less than a decade of continuous work experience. In Chapter 4, age and experience profiles of earnings and wage rates are distinguished and compared among

---

3. Some of them are surveyed in Reder (1969) and Mincer (1970).

4. For a corresponding human capital analysis of female earnings, see Mincer and Polachek (1974).

different schooling groups. Inferences about intergroup differences in investment behavior and in wages flow from the analysis of experience profiles.

Chapter 5 contains an empirical specification and application in regression form of a simple version of the human capital earnings function. This version includes only three independent variables: years of schooling, years of work experience, and weeks worked during the year. Estimates derived from this earnings function showed substantial explanatory power in a statistical and qualitative sense.

Chapter 6 contains a study of residuals from the regressions of Chapter 5. Patterns of observed variances and skewness parameters within schooling-experience groups are analyzed in the light of the human capital model.

In Chapter 7, the human capital analysis is contrasted with "random shock" models. Tests of discrimination are performed on Consumers Union panel data. Further, there is an analysis of the effects of intensive and extensive aggregation of data on earnings inequality, "intensive" referring to aggregation of personal into family income and "extensive" to wider coverage of population groups. At the level of detail in the current study, the empirical predictions of the human capital model are not substantially changed by such aggregations.

Chapter 8 contains a summary of major findings of the study, a discussion of their limitations, and an agenda for more comprehensive research.

Part I

THEORETICAL ANALYSIS

1

Individual Acquisition of Earning Power

Investments in people are time consuming. Each additional period of schooling or job training postpones the time of the individual's receipt of earnings and reduces the span of his working life, if he retires at a fixed age. The deferral of earnings and the possible reduction of earning life are costly. These time costs plus direct money outlays make up the total cost of investment. Because of these costs investment is not undertaken unless it raises the level of the deferred income stream. Hence, at the time it is undertaken, the present value of real earnings streams with and without investment are equal only at a positive discount rate. This rate is the internal rate of return on the investment.

For simplicity the rate of return is often treated as a parameter for the individual. This amounts to assuming that a change in an individual's investment does not change his marginal (hence average) rate of return. Another empirically convenient assumption is that all investment costs are time costs. This assumption is more realistic in such forms of human capital investments as on-the-job training, but less so in others, such as schooling, migration, or investments in health. In calculating schooling costs, an equivalent assumption is that students' direct private costs are exactly offset by their part-time earnings during the year.[1] Like the preceding one, this assumption is not essential. Detailed information on direct costs can be incorporated into the model to yield a more precise empirical analysis. We forego precision, in order to gain in the simplicity of exposition and analysis.

The first step is to analyze the effects of investments in schooling. This is done by assuming that no further human capital investments are undertaken after completion of schooling and also, at this stage, that the flow of individual earnings is constant throughout the working life. For this the cessation of net investment is a necessary, but not sufficient, condition. Also excluded are economywide changes affecting individual productivity and earnings during the life cycle.

Since changes in earnings are produced by *net* investments in human capital stock, the net concept is used in most of the analysis. In this section, zero depreciation is, in effect, assumed during the school years and zero net investment during the working life. These assumptions are amended in later sections and in empirical interpretations.

In specifying the lengths of earning lives it is first assumed that each additional year of schooling reduces earning life by exactly one year. An alternative, and mathematically simpler, formulation is one in which the span of earning life remains the same in all cases, with more educated people retiring at correspondingly later ages. Empirically, this assumption is more nearly the correct one.[2]

---

1. This assumption was defended and used by Hanoch (1967, pp. 317–320).

2. More educated men retire later. The length of working life is roughly constant. Only after high school does an additional year of schooling reduce earning life somewhat (by less than half a year).

The following table contains estimates of the average "retirement" age and length of working life of men classified by level of schooling. It is based on a March 1970 BLS labor force survey (1970b, Table E, p. A-11). Very similar estimates are produced from data in years before 1970.

Years of Schooling	Estimated Average Retirement Age	Estimated Length of Working Life
8	65	47
9–11	66	47
12	67	47
13–15	67	45
16	68	45
17 or more	70	45

(*note continued*)

When earning life is long, the alternative formulations cannot make much of a difference. What matters is the deferral of earnings: The cost of currently postponing earnings by one year is much more significant than the present cost of reducing earnings by one year, four or five decades hence. An infinite earning life can, of course, be viewed as a special case of the equal-span assumption. The advantage of the latter formulation is both its greater tractability and its flexibility in empirical interpretation.

1.1   THE SCHOOLING MODEL

In calculating the effects of schooling on earnings, it is first assumed that postponement of earnings due to lengthier schooling is tantamount to a reduction of the earning span.

Let

n = length of working life plus length of schooling

= length of working life for persons without schooling

Y_s = annual earnings of an individual with s years of schooling

V_s = present value of an individual's lifetime earnings at start of schooling

r = discount rate

t = 0, 1, 2, . . . , n time, in years

d = difference in the amount of schooling, in years

e = base of natural logarithms

Then

$$V_s = Y_s \sum_{t=s+1}^{n} \left(\frac{1}{1+r}\right)^t,$$

(*Note 2 concluded*)

Estimates of retirement age are obtained by adding to age 45 the product of participation rates and years beyond the age of 45. The length of working life is the sum of products of participation rates and age intervals.

Estimates of lengths of working life in eight broad occupational groups, based on 1930–50 Census data, suggested larger differences in the earning spans among occupations. Note, however, that because of occupational mobility, length of stay in an occupational class, even when that is broadly defined, is not coextensive with length of stay in the labor force. Compare Mincer (1958, p. 284, n. 12).

The finding that the length of earning life of more educated men is the same as that of the less educated is not inconsistent with the observed positive relation between schooling and labor force participation at the middle and older ages (Bowen and Finnegan, 1969): A negative relation holds when the more educated are still at school.

when the discounting process is discrete. And, more conveniently, when the process is continuous:

$$V_s = Y_s \int_s^n e^{-rt}dt = \frac{Y_s(e^{-rs} - e^{-rn})}{r}.$$

Similarly, the present value of lifetime earnings of an individual who engages in $s - d$ years of schooling is:

$$V_{s-d} = \frac{Y_{s-d}}{r} (e^{-r(s-d)} - e^{-rn}).$$

The ratio, $k_{s,s-d}$, of annual earnings after s years to earnings after $s - d$ years of schooling is found by letting $V_s = V_{s-d}$:

$$k_{s,s-d} = \frac{Y_s}{Y_{s-d}} = \frac{e^{-r(s-d)} - e^{-rn}}{e^{-rs} - e^{-rn}} = \frac{e^{r(n+d-s)} - 1}{e^{r(n-s)} - 1}. \tag{1.1}$$

It is easily seen that $k_{s,s-d}$ is (1) larger than unity, (2) a positive function of r, (3) a negative function of n. In other words, (1) people with more schooling command higher annual pay; (2) the difference between earnings of individuals due to the difference in investment of d years of schooling is larger the higher the rate of return on schooling; (3) the difference is larger the shorter the general span of working life, since the costs of schooling must be recouped over a *relatively* shorter period.

These conclusions are quite obvious. Less obvious is the finding that $k_{s,s-d}$ is a positive function of s (d fixed); that is, relative income differences between, for example, persons with 10 years and 8 years of schooling are larger than those between individuals with 4 and 2 years of schooling, respectively. However, since the change in $k_{s,s-d}$ with a change in s and n is negligible[3] when n is large, it can be, for all practical purposes, treated as a constant, k.

The conclusion that k is constant holds exactly when spans of

---

3.
$$\frac{\partial k}{\partial s} = \frac{r[e^{r(n+d-s)} - e^{r(n-s)}]}{[e^{r(n-s)} - 1]^2} > 0; \quad \frac{\partial k}{\partial s} \to 0, \text{ when } n \to \infty;$$

$$\frac{\partial k}{\partial n} = \frac{r[e^{r(n-s)} - e^{r(n+d-s)}]}{[e^{r(n-s)} - 1]^2} > 0; \quad \frac{\partial k}{\partial n} \to 0, \text{ when } n \to \infty.$$

Both partial derivatives are numerically very small when r and n are in a wide neighborhood of 0.10 and 40, respectively.

earning life are assumed fixed, regardless of schooling. Redefine n as the fixed span of earning life.

Then

$$V_s = Y_s \int_s^{n+s} e^{-rt} dt = \frac{Y_s}{r} e^{-rs}(1 - e^{-rn});$$

$$V_{s-d} = Y_{s-d} \int_{s-d}^{n+s-d} e^{-rt} dt = \frac{Y_{s-d}}{r} (1 - e^{-rn}) e^{-r(s-d)};$$

and solving for $k_{s,s-d}$ from the equalization of present values, we get:

$$k_{s,s-d} = \frac{Y_s}{Y_{s-d}} = \frac{e^{-r(s-d)}}{e^{-rs}} = e^{rd}. \tag{1.2}$$

Here, in contrast to (1.1) the earnings ratio, k, of incomes differing by d years of schooling does not at all depend on the level of schooling (s) nor, more interestingly, on the length of earning life (n), when that is finite, even if short.

Now, define $k_{s,0} = Y_s/Y_0 = k_s$. By (1.2), $k_s = e^{rs}$. In logarithms the formula becomes:

$$\ln Y_s = \ln Y_0 + rs. \tag{1.3}$$

Equation (1.3) exhibits the basic conclusion that percentage increments in earnings are strictly proportional to the absolute differences in the time spent at school, with the rate of return as the coefficient of proportionality. More precisely, equation (1.3) shows the logarithm of earnings to be a strict linear function of time spent at school.

1.2   POST-SCHOOL INVESTMENTS: INDIVIDUAL EARNINGS PROFILES

The "schooling model" represented by equation (1.3) is the most primitive form of a human capital earnings function: Y_s in (1.3) is the level of earnings of persons who do not invest in human capital beyond s years of schooling. Since most individuals continue to develop their skills and earning capacity after completion of schooling, Y_s cannot be directly observed. Instead, an "earnings profile" is observed: the variation of earnings with age during the working life.

We proceed to a human capital analysis of the earnings profile, at first ignoring depreciation phenomena.

After entering the labor force in year j, the worker devotes resources C_j mainly in furthering his job skills and acquiring job-related information, whether in the form of direct dollar outlays or opportunity costs of time devoted to these purposes, on or off the job. His "net" earnings Y_j in year j are obtained, therefore, by deducting C_j dollars from his "gross" earnings or "earnings capacity" E_j, which he would earn if he did not continue to invest in himself.[4]

Accordingly, earnings during the first year of work experience, $j = 0$, are $Y_0 = Y_s - C_0$, where $Y_s (= E_s)$ is the initial earning capacity after completion of s years of schooling.

If investment ceased subsequently, earnings in the next year (and afterward) would be: $Y_1 = Y_s + r_0C_0$. However, if investment in that year is C_1, then $Y_1 = Y_s + r_0C_0 - C_1$. More generally, net earnings in year j are:

$$Y_j = Y_s + \sum_{t=0}^{j-1} r_tC_t - C_j = E_j - C_j. \tag{1.4}$$

The generality of expression (1.4) is evident, since the start of index t is essentially arbitrary. In Becker's original statement of the accounting equation (1.4), Y_0 replaces Y_s; and in instalments C_t, schooling and post-school investments are not distinguished. In fact, the expression for Y_s, the schooling model, is a special case of (1.4), in which investments are restricted to time costs of schooling and rates of return are the same in all periods. Then, with $C_t = E_t$:

$$E_s = Y_0 + r \sum_{t=1}^{s} E_{t-1} = Y_0(1 + r)^s, \tag{1.5}$$

which is a discrete approximation of (1.3).

Using equation (1.4) we can proceed to the analysis of variation of earnings over the working life.[5] On the assumption that working

---

4. Note that observed earnings, as they are usually reported, would equal "net" earnings if C_j consisted of opportunity costs only. However, direct costs are included in reported earnings. Thus observed earnings overstate "net" earnings, but since direct costs are much smaller than opportunity costs, observed earnings more closely approximate Y_j than E_j.

5. At this point we are abstracting from variations in hours or weeks of labor supplied over the life cycle. Some consideration is given to this factor later.

life starts in the period following the completion of schooling, equation (1.4) points to post-school investments C_j as the variable which traces out the individual "age profile" of earnings. The initial earning capacity Y_s acquired in years of schooling s is taken as constant for a given individual, though it may vary among individuals. Y_s is not readily observed, since most or all individuals are assumed to engage in post-school investment of one form or another.

The variation of earnings with experience is best observed by considering the annual increment of earnings in (1.4):

$$\Delta Y_j = Y_{j+1} - Y_j = r_j C_j - (C_{j+1} - C_j). \tag{1.6}$$

According to (1.6), earnings grow with experience so long as net investment (C_j) is positive and its annual instalments either diminish $[(C_{j+1} - C_j) < 0]$ or increase at a rate lower than the rate of return:

$$\text{for } \Delta Y_j > 0, \ \frac{C_{j+1} - C_j}{C_j} < r_j.$$

Note that if investments increase sharply (at a faster rate than r), net earnings will decline, presumably temporarily. However, gross earnings always increase, so long as investment is positive, since

$$\Delta E_j = r_j C_j. \tag{1.7}$$

If both r_j and investment are the same in all periods ($C_j = C_{j+1}$; $r_j = r$), net and gross earnings grow linearly. Henceforth we shall assume that all $r_j = r$.

While constant or linearly increasing investment C_j is conceivable for some stages of individual work experience, these assumptions cannot be expected to hold over any long periods of the working life. Such assumptions are inconsistent with the theory of optimal allocation of investment in human capital over the life cycle. Rational allocation requires that most of the investment be undertaken at younger ages. Thus schooling, a largely full-time activity, precedes job-training, a largely part-time activity, and the latter diminishes with age, terminating years before retirement.

According to Becker (1964 and 1967) this tendency is due to the following incentives for shifting from learning to earning activities as soon as possible: (1) With finite lifetimes, later investments produce returns over a shorter period; so total benefits are smaller. (2) To the extent that investments in human capital are profitable, their postponement reduces the present value of net gains. (3) A person's time is an important input in his investment, but the consequence of human capital accumulation is an increase in the value of his time; thus investments at later periods are more costly, because forgone earnings (per hour) increase. However, these incentives would be overridden in the special or temporary cases where productivity in learning grows as fast or faster than productivity in earning.

Should we then not expect an early and quick accumulation of all the desired human capital even before individuals begin their working life? The answer of human capital theory to this question is twofold: Investments are spread out over time because the marginal cost curve of producing them is upward sloping within each period. They decline over time both because marginal benefits decline and because the marginal cost curve shifts upward.

Specifically, the argument (Ben-Porath, 1967; Becker, 1967) visualizes individuals as firms which produce additions (Q) to their own human capital stock (H) by combining their human capital with their own time (T) and with other market resources (R) in a production function:

$$Q = f(H, T, R).$$

Attempts to increase investments Q within a given period run into diminishing returns: Costs rise with the speed of production. Thus the marginal cost curve in Figure 1.1 is upward sloping.

The marginal revenue obtained by adding a unit of investment to the capital stock is the discounted flow of future increases in earning power. For reasons indicated, the benefits of later investments decline. The MR curve slides downward with increasing age, tracing out a declining pattern of investment over the life cycle.

The decline is reinforced if the MC curve shifts to the left with advancing age. As already mentioned, this is not a logical necessity: MC would remain fixed if earning and learning powers increased at the same rate. A recent attempt by Ben-Porath (1970) to test for such "neutrality" empirically suggests that investments decline over earning life faster than would be predicted by the mere downward slide of MR on a fixed MC curve in Figure 1.1. By implication, marginal costs rise over the life cycle.

Investments, however, need not decline throughout the life cycle. Ben-Porath (1967) has shown that the optimization process

FIGURE 1.1
PRODUCTION OF HUMAN CAPITAL

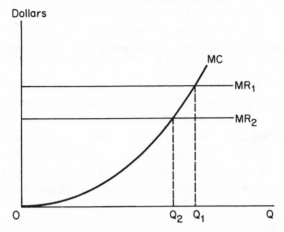

may lead to an increase in investment during the early stages because of "corner solutions": The initial stock (H_0) may be so small that even an input of all the available time, other resources not being highly substitutable, produces less than the optimal amount of output. As the stock increases, investment output will increase for a while until an optimum is reached with an input of less than the total available time. At this point investments and the time devoted to them begin to decline. The initial period of complete specialization in the production of human capital is devoted to full-time schooling. It is identified by the absence of earnings, a condition which may end before the completion of schooling.

The optimization process described above applies explicitly (Ben-Porath, 1967) to gross investments in human capital. Note, however, that the predicted decline in gross investment applies a fortiori to net investment if depreciation is constant or increases with age.

Two major conclusions can be drawn from the Ben-Porath analysis:

1. The higher the marginal revenue curve and the lower the marginal cost curve (cf. Figure 1.1), the larger the investment in human capital in any given period. Marginal revenue is higher the lower the discount rate and the depreciation rate, and the longer the expected length of working life. Marginal cost is lower, the greater the learning

ability of the individual. Since the nature and conditions of individuals which these factors describe change rather slowly, the size of single-period investments is likely to be an index of lifetime investments. Longer schooling is likely to be followed by greater post-school investment, and generally, the serial correlation of instalments of investment is likely to be positive.

2. While the preceding inference is significant for a distributional analysis, the major implication of Ben-Porath's optimization analysis for the individual investment profile is that investment costs can be expected to decline after the schooling stage. As a result, both gross and net earnings slope upward during the positive net investment period. Moreover, the age profile of gross earnings is concave from below. From (1.7), we have the second difference:

$$\Delta^2 E_j = r\Delta C_j < 0, \tag{1.8}$$

since $\Delta C_j < 0$. Net earnings need not be concave throughout. The profile is concave if the decline of investments (C_j) is a nonincreasing function of j, i.e., if

$$\Delta^2 Y_j = r\Delta C_j - \Delta^2 C_j < 0. \tag{1.9}$$

If investments decline at a strongly increasing rate for a while, so that the inequality sign is reversed, age profiles may rise at an accelerating rate for a while; but eventually they become concave as net investment terminates.

The profile of net earnings has a steeper slope than gross earnings, since $\Delta Y_j = \Delta E_j - \Delta C_j$, and $\Delta C_j < 0$. The peak of both gross and net earnings is reached when positive net investments equal zero.[6]

Figure 1.2 indicates the shape of gross earnings E_j and net earnings Y_j during the post-school investment period OP. Of particular interest are the initial earnings capacity Y_s and peak earnings Y_p. The former, Y_s, is the earnings concept used in the schooling model. Its estimate is particularly useful for the empirical analyses in this study. Estimates of Y_s and of Y_p would make possible quick and simple methods of estimating rates of return and amounts of investment costs.

During the early years of experience, earnings of continuing in-

---

6. I abstract from depreciation and from changing hours of work.

FIGURE 1.2
EARNINGS PROFILES

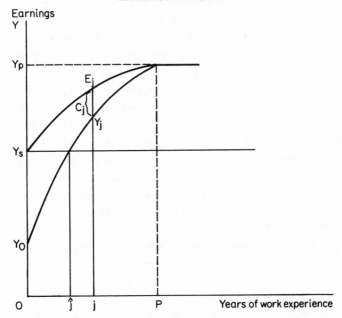

vestors are smaller than the Y_s earnings that can be obtained after s years of schooling without further investments. But earnings of investors continue to grow and, before long, exceed Y_s. In Figure 1.2, $\hat{j}$ is the overtaking year of experience. Knowledge of $\hat{j}$ permits one to read off the value Y_s from the profile of observed earnings Y_j. It turns out that $\hat{j}$ is an early stage of experience, and its upper limit can be estimated from equation (1.4):

$$Y_{\hat{j}} = Y_s + r \sum_{t=0}^{j-1} C_t - C_j = Y_s, \quad \text{when} \quad \sum_{t=0}^{j-1} C_t = C_j.$$

If instalments C_t from $t = 0$ to $t = \hat{j}$ are equal, then $r\hat{j}C_j = C_j$; so $\hat{j} = 1/r$. If C_t declines, $\hat{j}$ is reached sooner; therefore, assume C_t is not increasing. Then,

$$\hat{j} \le \frac{1}{r}. \tag{1.10}$$

To illustrate, if r exceeds 10 per cent, it takes less than a decade for the trained person to overtake the untrained one, if both start their working life with the same initial earning capacity.

Even for the rough estimate of Y_s by (1.10) it is necessary to know the value of r_p, the rate of return to post-school investment. If r_p is known, Y_s can be more precisely determined, since at the start of working life the present value of the constant earnings stream Y_s must equal the present value of the observed earnings profile Y_j, with r_p as the discount rate. If, as is perforce assumed in empirical calculations of rates of return to "education," the rate of return to post-school investment (r_p) equals r_s, the rate of return to schooling, the conventionally calculated rates can be applied to estimate Y_s. In turn, estimates of Y_s at two levels s_1 and s_2 make it possible to apply a check of internal consistency to the hypothesized equality $r_s = r_p$, since, by (1.3) $\ln Y_{s2} - \ln Y_{s1} = r_s(s_2 - s_1)$. Further applications of the "overtaking" or "crossover" point of the earnings profile to short-cut estimation of changes in rates of return and to distributional analysis are elaborated in Part II of this study.

At the end of the net investment period,

$$Y_p = Y_s + r_p \sum_{t=0}^{p} C_t. \tag{1.11}$$

The total volume of post-school investment costs $\sum_{t=0}^{p} C_t$ can be estimated, once r_p, hence Y_s, are known,[7] since

$$\sum_{t=0}^{p} C_t = \frac{Y_p - Y_s}{r_p}. \tag{1.12}$$

Similarly, the costs of rising from schooling level s_1 to level s_2 are:

$$\sum_{s_1}^{s_2} C_s = \frac{Y_{s2} - Y_{s1}}{r_s}. \tag{1.13}$$

The above analysis of dollar profiles of earnings is easily translated into an analysis of logarithmic earnings profiles. This is not only useful but necessary, for two reasons: (1) Relative (percentage) variation in earnings is of major interest in the study of income inequality; and (2) for empirical analysis, post-school investments must be expressed in the same "time" units as schooling. Indeed, the conversion of investment costs into time-equivalent values trans-

---

7. In Figure 1.2, total post-school investment costs are given by the area $Y_0 Y_s Y_p$.

forms the earnings equation (1.4) into its logarithmic version. This is accomplished by the following device: [8]

Let k_j be the ratio of investment costs C_j to gross earnings E_j in period j. This ratio can be viewed as the fraction of time (or "time-equivalent," if investment costs include direct outlays as well as time costs) the worker devotes to the improvement of his earning power. His net earnings in year j are, therefore, smaller by this fraction than they would be if he did not invest during year j:

$$C_j = k_j E_j,$$

and

$$E_j = E_{j-1} + rC_{j-1} = E_{j-1}(1 + rk_{j-1}).$$

By recursion, therefore:

$$E_j = E_0 \prod_{t=0}^{j-1} (1 + r_t k_t).$$

Assuming $k \leq 1$ and r relatively small, this is approximately:

$$\ln E_j = \ln E_0 + \sum_{t=0}^{j-1} r_t k_t; \qquad (1.14)$$

and since $Y_j = E_j(1 - k_j)$, we get

$$\ln Y_j = \ln E_0 + \sum_{t=0}^{j-1} r_t k_t + \ln (1 - k_j). \qquad (1.15)$$

The assumption that $k_j = 1$ during the school years shows (1.15) to be an expansion of the schooling model:

$$\ln Y_j = \ln E_0 + r_s s + r_p \sum_{t=0}^{j-1} k_t + \ln (1 - k_j). \qquad (1.16)$$

The assumption that r_j is the same for all post-school investments simplifies matters. Let

$$K_j = \sum_{t=0}^{j-1} k_t,$$

the cumulative amount of "time" expended in post-school investments before year j. Then

$$\ln E_j = \ln E_0 + r_s s + r_p K_j = \ln Y_s + r_p K_j. \qquad (1.17)$$

---

8. This device was applied by Becker and Chiswick (1966) to schooling investment. Here it is extended to cover post-school investments.

If $r_s = r_p$, we have, denoting $h_j = (s + K_j)$, the simplest generalization of the schooling model:

$$\ln E_j = \ln E_0 + rh_j. \tag{1.18}$$

When the investment period is completed, K_p is total "time" devoted to post-school investment. It can be calculated from (1.17), if r_p is known:

$$K_p = \frac{\ln Y_p - \ln Y_s}{r_p}. \tag{1.19}$$

The earnings profiles under these assumptions provide information on the number of "years" of post-school "training," a statistic that is impossible to obtain in surveys of workers or firms, and one that is bound to be greatly underestimated if it is based on reported apprenticeship periods or other formal training programs in firms.[9]

The shape of the log-earnings profile is upward sloping so long as $k_j > 0$. Its rate of growth and concavity are given by the first and second derivative of (1.15) with the same conclusions as in the dollar profiles, with k_j replacing C_j.

Note that the decline in k_j with experience follows a fortiori from the assumption of declining dollar values of post-school investments, and that consequently concavity in the logarithmic profile is to be expected more frequently, that is, even when the dollar profile is linear or S-shaped.

In the foregoing analysis it was assumed that (1) net investment is never negative, that is, the formulation abstracts from depreciation phenomena; and (2) changes in earnings over the life cycle represent changes in earning capacity rather than changes in hours of work supplied to the labor market (including the hours spent in on-the-job training).

The first assumption is not seriously misleading in the life-cycle context if the second is maintained: As Chart 4.4 in Part II shows, "full-time" earnings or wage rates reach a peak and remain on a plateau until men reach an age near retirement. On average (the data are mean earnings classified by years of education), net investment may be viewed as non-negative through most of the working life. Still, the finiteness of life, the increasing incidence of illness at older

---

9. Cf. discussion in Mincer (1962). Of course K_p includes forms of investment other than post-school training. Information and job mobility are examples.

ages, and the secular progress of knowledge, which makes older education and skill vintages obsolescent, are compelling facts suggesting that as age advances, effects of depreciation eventually begin to outstrip gross investment.

To accommodate these phenomena the formulation is amended by positing a rate δ_t at which the human capital stock H_t depreciates in time period t. Then

$$E_t = E_{t-1} + rC^*_{t-1} - \delta_{t-1}E_{t-1}, \tag{1.20}$$

where C^*_t denotes gross investment, as C_t denoted net investment. Letting the gross investment ratio $k^*_t = C^*_t/E_t$, we get:

$$\frac{E_t}{E_{t-1}} = 1 + rk^*_{t-1} - \delta_{t-1} = 1 + rk_{t-1};$$

thus $k_t = [k^*_t - (\delta_t/r)]$, and

$$\ln E_t = \ln E_{t-1} + \ln (1 + rk^*_{t-1} - \delta_{t-1})$$

by recursion, and assuming $(rk^*_t - \delta_t)$ is small, we have:

$$\ln E_t = \ln E_0 + \sum_{j=0}^{t-1} (rk^*_j - \delta_j), \tag{1.21}$$

and

$$\ln Y_t = \ln E_t + \ln (1 - k^*_t) \tag{1.22}$$

as an amendment to (1.14). It is clear that the peak of earning capacity E_t is reached when $k_t = 0$, i.e., when $k^*_t = \delta_t/r$; call it $k^*(E \text{ max})$. It is also clear that observed wage rates reach a peak some time thereafter, since from (1.22):

$$\ln Y_t = \ln Y_{t-1} + \ln (1 + rk^*_{t-1} - \delta_{t-1}) + \ln (1 - k^*_t) - \ln (1 - k^*_{t-1}) = 0 \tag{1.23}$$

only when $rk^*_{t-1} < \delta_{t-1}$, i.e., when net investment is negative. It can be shown [10] that if δ is fixed and if the gross investment ratio k^*_t declines

---

10. From (1.23) Y_t reaches a maximum when, approximately

$$rk^*_{t-1} - \delta = k^*_t - k^*_{t-1}.$$

Then

$$r[k^*_{t-1} - k^*(E \text{ max})] = k^*_t - k^*_{t-1}$$

and

$$\hat{t} = \frac{k^*(E \text{ max}) - k^*_{t-1}}{k^*_{t-1} - k^*_t} = \frac{1}{r}.$$

linearly over time, the (unobservable) peak of earning capacity precedes the (observed) peak of wage rates by $\hat{t} = 1/r$, that is, by about a decade or even earlier if the rate of decline of k_t^* diminishes over the life cycle. Note, also, that while the net investment period terminates before peak earnings (wage rates) are observed, the gross investment period continues beyond it.

In a few recent human capital analyses in which depreciation is taken into account, the rate is assumed to be fixed purely for mathematical convenience.[11] Yet, the depreciation rate on human capital is likely to be related to age, experience, and size and vintage of stock. If descriptions in developmental psychology can serve as a guide, the life-cycle pattern of δ_t after the individual matures is plausibly described as flat and very low, beginning to rise in the fifties.[12]

To the extent that hours of work vary over the life cycle, the profile of annual earnings is affected. Under conditions of certainty, for example, individual wealth can be considered fixed, while the cost of time grows with experience until peak earning capacity is reached. If so, the growth and decline of earning capacity is likely to induce a corresponding pattern of hours of work supplied to the market. Hence, the growth of observed *annual* earnings leads to overestimates of investments in human capital or of rates of return. Hours of

---

11. Cf. Johnson (1970), Rosen (1974), and Koeune (1972).

12. Health statistics show the proportions of workers with some limitations of work activities during the year to be rising slowly to 13 per cent of those in the 45–54 age range, and accelerating to 55 per cent at age 75. However, in a survey of the psychological literature, Birren (1968, pp. 180–181) states: "Except for individuals with cumulative injuries or problems of health, worker performance up to age 60 should be little influenced by *physiological* changes in aging." In discussing age changes in *learning capacity*, the same author states: "There has been a general tendency since the work of E. L. Thorndike in the 1920's to advance continually the age at which subjects in learning research are regarded as aged. At the present time there is little evidence to suggest that there is an intrinsic age difference in learning capacity over the employed years, i.e. up to age 60."

Psychologists note, of course, that it is difficult empirically to isolate *intrinsic* age patterns in productivity, that is, changes that are not affected by the individual's adaptation, such as health care and training — gross investment, in our terminology. Hence, their observations of time changes in "productive capacity" often show systematic differences when individuals are stratified by education, social background, ability measures, and so forth. [See Mincer (1957, Chap. 1, n. 1).] To the extent that these patterns reflect differential patterns of "adaptation," the analysis of human capital investment behavior is likely to contribute to an understanding of these findings, rather than conversely.

work may peak before observed wage rates because, as noted above (cf. note 10), capacity wage rates decline before observed wage rates do, given human capital depreciation.[13]

Variation in hours (weeks) worked is taken account of in the empirical analyses. The analysis of the relation between hours of work and human capital investments is not theoretically integrated into the present model. Though the problem is discussed in several places below, its fuller development is relegated to a future study.

---

13. Recent analyses of optimal allocation of consumption and work over the life cycle by Becker and Ghez (1967 and 1972) suggest that hours of work are likely to peak before earning capacity, a fortiori before observed wage rates decline.

2

Distribution Analysis

2.1 THE SCHOOLING MODEL

The analysis of individual earnings is now adapted to a cross section of workers. I begin with schooling, that is, I restrict human capital investment to schooling alone. In equation (2.1) a subscript i is now attached to the variables Y (earnings) and s (years of schooling) in order to distinguish individual differences in them. For simplicity, I initially disregard individual differences in the (average) rate of return r and in original earning capacity Y_0. The symbol Y_s denotes hypothetical earnings of an individual who does not continue to invest in human capital after the completion of s years of schooling.

$$\ln Y_{si} = \ln Y_0 + r s_i. \tag{2.1}$$

Even at this primitive stage, several important and rather realistic implications follow for the personal distribution of earnings:

1. The positive skewness that is almost always exhibited by distributions of income or earnings may be partly due to the effect of the logarithmic transformation, which converts absolute differences in schooling into percentage differences in earnings. Clearly,

a symmetric distribution of schooling implies a positively skewed distribution of earnings. Indeed, a positive skew of earnings cannot be avoided unless the distribution of schooling is strongly skewed in the negative direction.

2. The larger the dispersion in the distribution of schooling, the larger the relative dispersion and skewness in the distribution of earnings.

3. The higher the rate of return to schooling, the larger the earnings inequality and skewness.

The implications for inequality are shown by taking variances in equation (2.1), assuming both Y_0 and r to be fixed:

$$\sigma^2(\ln Y_s) = r^2\sigma^2(s). \tag{2.2}$$

The implications for skewness are shown most simply in a non-parametric formulation: Let Y_1 be a lower percentile level of earnings corresponding to an s_1 level of schooling; Y_2, symmetric upper percentile corresponding to s_2; Y_m, median earnings; and s_m, median schooling.

Assume first a symmetric distribution of schooling, so that $s_2 - s_m = s_m - s_1 = d$. The absolute (dollar) dispersion in the earnings distribution is $D = Y_2 - Y_1 = (e^{2rd} - 1)Y_1$; so $Y_2 = e^{2rd}Y_1$. The relative dispersion $RD = Y_2/Y_1 = e^{2rd}$. Positive skewness exists when $(Y_1 + Y_2)/2 > Y_m$. A measure of it is

$$Sk = \tfrac{1}{2}(Y_2 - 2Y_m + Y_1) = \tfrac{1}{2}(e^{2rd} - 2e^{rd} + 1)Y_1$$

$$= \tfrac{1}{2}(e^{rd} - 1)^2 Y_1 > 0.$$

Using Bowley's formula, relative skewness is defined as,

$$RSk = \frac{(Y_2 - Y_m) - (Y_m - Y_1)}{Y_2 - Y_1} = \frac{Sk}{\tfrac{1}{2}(Y_2 - Y_1)} = \frac{(e^{rd} - 1)^2}{e^{2rd} - 1} = \frac{e^{rd} - 1}{e^{rd} + 1} > 0. \tag{2.3}$$

Both measures of skewness are necessarily positive, and all measures of dispersion and skewness are positive functions of the dispersion in the distribution of schooling (d) and of the rate of return on investment in schooling (r).

These conclusions remain unchanged when the distribution of schooling is not symmetric, except that the degree of skewness in the earnings distribution is now additionally affected by the degree of skewness in the distribution of schooling. Let $s_2 - s_m = d_2$; and $s_m - s_1 = d_1$; $d_2 \neq d_1$. Then

$$s_k = Y_2 - 2Y_m + Y_1 = [e^{r(d_1+d_2)} - 2e^{rd_1} + 1]Y_1. \tag{2.4}$$

Let $d_2 = d_1 + \Delta$.

Let relative skewness in the distribution of schooling be defined by $sks = \Delta/d_1$. Then it can be shown (by approximation [1]) that even when sks is negative, the distribution of earnings remains positively skewed when the absolute value of sks does not exceed rd_1 and the latter is less than unity:

$$\frac{d_1 - d_2}{d_1} < rd_1 < 1. \tag{2.5}$$

The empirical usefulness of the schooling model formulated in equation (2.1) may be questioned on two grounds: The initial earnings level Y_0 and the rate of return r cannot be assumed to be the same at all levels of schooling and for all persons. It is merely a convenient simplifying assumption. But if individual values of r are independent of s, and (2.1) is used as a statistical estimating equation, then r must be thought of as an average over all schooling levels and

---

1. Skewness in the distribution of earnings is positive when

$$e^{2rd_1+r\Delta} - 2e^{rd_1} + 1 > 0$$

or

$$(e^{rd_1} - 1)^2 + e^{2rd_1}(e^{r\Delta} - 1) > 0; \quad (e^{rd_1} - 1)^2 > e^{2rd_1}(1 - e^{r\Delta})$$

when $\Delta < 0$, $1 - e^{r\Delta} > 0$.

Taking square roots:

$$e^{rd_1} - 1 > e^{rd_1}\sqrt{1 - e^{r\Delta}}; \quad e^{rd_1} > \frac{1}{1 - \sqrt{1 - e^{r\Delta}}}.$$

Taking logs: $rd_1 > -\ln(1 - \sqrt{1 - e^{r\Delta}})$. This condition holds when $rd_1 > \sqrt{1 - e^{r\Delta}}$, since for $x < 1$, $x > -\ln(1 - x)$, by the Taylor expansion. Hence $e^{r\Delta} > 1 - r^2d_1^2$ is a sufficient condition for positive skewness in earnings when $\Delta < 0$.

Again, assuming $r^2d_1^2$ sufficiently small, and taking logs, $r\Delta > -r^2d_1^2$, and so $|\Delta/d_1| < rd_1 < 1$ is a sufficient condition for positive skewness in earnings, when $\Delta < 0$.

This condition can also be written as $rd_2 > rd_1(1 - rd_1)$. It is always fulfilled when $rd_2 > 0.25$, so long as $rd_1 < 1$. Skewness was defined with respect to a particular $(s_1 - s_2)$ interval in the distribution of schooling. Therefore, so long as an s_2 can be found such that $r(s_2 - s_m) > 0.25$, where s_m is median schooling, the distribution of earnings must be positively skewed in that interval.

persons, and individual differences in r (and in ln Y_0) are impounded in the statistical residual.

Let rates of return differ by schooling level. Then equation (2.1) becomes

$$\ln Y_s = \ln Y_0 + \sum_{t=1}^{s} r_t = \ln Y_0 + \bar{r}s,$$

where r_t is the marginal rate of return for a particular level of schooling, and $\bar{r}$ is the average. If $\bar{r}$ is not the same for all individuals (i), then

$$\ln Y_{si} = \ln Y_{0i} + \bar{r}_i s_i. \tag{2.6}$$

Now the inequality of earnings in a group is affected not only by the dispersion in schooling and by the average size of the rate of return, as indicated by equation (2.2), but also by the dispersion in the rates of return and by the average level of schooling. This is clearly seen in the case where $\bar{r}_i$ and s_i are independent.[2] Ignoring variation in Y_0:

$$\sigma^2(\ln Y_s) = \bar{r}^2\sigma^2(s) + \bar{s}^2\sigma^2(r) + \sigma^2(s)\sigma^2(r). \tag{2.7}$$

Here $\bar{r}$ is the average of $\bar{r}_i$ across individuals.

Should it not be assumed that $\bar{r}_i$ and s_i are positively related? Presumably, persons who can benefit more (get larger returns) from given amounts of investment will invest more. However, the average rate of return of an individual, $\bar{r}_i$, ceases to be an index of his ability to benefit from schooling investment when individuals with differing amounts of investment are compared, because $\bar{r}_i$ depends, in part, on the level of investment. As spelled out by Becker (1967), the condition for a positive correlation between $\bar{r}_i$ and s_i in a cross section is that the dispersion of "abilities" (levels of demand curves for investment funds) exceed the dispersion of "opportunities" (levels of investment fund supply curves).

There are no a priori reasons for specifying which dispersion is greater, and the empirical evidence [3] suggests there is little if any correlation between rates of return and quantities invested across

---

2. By a theorem of L. Goodman (1960).

3. See Tables 3.3 and 4.4 in Part II. In bodies of data in which Y_{0i}, $\bar{r}_i$, and s_i are correlated, empirical estimates of the coefficient of $\bar{r}$ will be biased. In that case the expression for the inequality of earnings (2.7) will contain additional variance and covariance terms.

individuals. Hereafter, the symbol $\bar{r}$ will not be used. Instead, unless it is otherwise stated, r will denote the average rate of return.

By definition, the schooling model described in (2.1) applies to the earnings of individuals who do not make post-school investments in human capital. Because such individuals are rare, these earnings cannot be directly observed. They can be rather crudely estimated, as explained in Chapter 1, by earnings at the overtaking stage of the life cycle (see Figure 1.2). In the following section, the earnings model is expanded beyond schooling to take account of variation in earnings due to life-cycle and individual differences in the distribution of post-school investments.

2.2   COMPARATIVE ANALYSIS OF EARNINGS PROFILES

Figure 2.1 portrays investment profiles of three individuals whose gross investment at each age is measured in "time-equivalent" units (k^*), that is, as a ratio to earning capacity. The three investment profiles $I_i = k^*_{ij}$ and a common depreciation curve $D = (\delta/r)_j$ are drawn schematically. Here i denotes the individual, j his age, δ the depreciation rate.

Individuals who invest more than others have their investment profiles shifted upward. I'_1 describes investment behavior of an individual with the same level of schooling (s_1) as I_1, but larger post-school investments while I_2 describes the investment profile of a person with more schooling (s_2) than I_1 but the same level of post-school investment as I'_1. I_1 and I_2 need not be parallel, but they are plausibly near-parallel, given that the expected period of gross investment T extends over most of a lifetime.

Consider now the two comparisons, and define experience as chronological time (j) since the start of post-school investments. Note that the net investment ratio k_j is given by the vertical difference between I and D, and recall that the growth rate of earning capacity in period j is given by rk_j.

If the increase in investment (from I_1 to I'_1) is restricted to post-school investment, meaning that *schooling* (s_1) is the same in both cases, then net investments (k_j) are larger for each additional year of *experience and of age,* and peak earning time (P_1) is shifted to a later age (P_2) and to a later year of experience. Earning capacity rises more rapidly at each age and for a longer period, reaching a higher level at P_2. Even if the increase in investment includes also an in-

FIGURE 2.1
AGE PROFILES OF INVESTMENT RATIOS

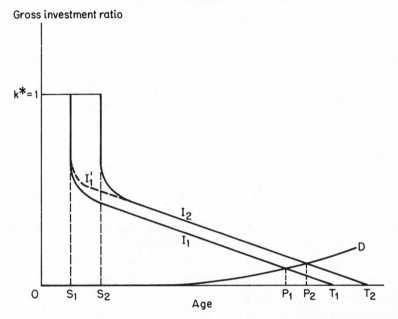

crease in schooling (shift from I_1 to I_2), the conclusion for the *age-earnings* profiles remains the same. This is not necessarily true, however, for the description of experience-earnings profiles, since the same age no longer represents the same year of experience as it did before. For example, if the shift from I_1 to I_2 is, indeed, parallel, as in Figure 2.1, meaning that *post-school gross investment* ratios remain unchanged, net investment ratios (k_j) will not be greater for each year of experience. In fact, they will actually be somewhat smaller if D has an upward slope; and peak earnings will be reached at an earlier year of experience. With D relatively flat, the (log) experience-earnings profiles are nearly parallel, though the age-earnings profiles diverge.[4]

---

4. This is exact when D is horizontal and the same in all schooling groups. Then the parallel shift of gross investment I_j implies the same parallel shift in net investments k_j. In that case, the logarithmic experience-earnings profiles would be exactly alike in the two cases, except for a difference in levels. At a given year of experience the ratio of earnings Y_{s_2+j}/Y_{s_1+j} would be equal to Y_{s_2}/Y_{s_1}. Thus, relative differentials in earnings between the two schooling groups would be the same at any level of experience, with or without post-school investments.

This analysis underscores the importance of distinguishing between age profiles and experience profiles of earnings. In the special case just discussed, shapes of experience profiles of (log) earnings are the same in all schooling groups, though shapes of age profiles are not. While relative intergroup differentials in earnings do not change with experience, they grow with age! This is because at given ages, earnings rise less rapidly (and decline more rapidly at advanced ages) for the lower profiles. For groups with more schooling earnings peak at the same or earlier years of experience, but at later ages.

If an increase in investment ratios results from both longer schooling and more "time" spent in post-school investments, that is, $s_2 > s_1$ and $k_{2j} > k_{1j}$ for each j, then log earnings profiles for both age and experience will be steeper and peak later than if either schooling or post-school investment are the same, though this behavior will be less evident in the latter profiles than in the former.

Note also that the steeper the upward slope of D in the neighborhood of its intersection with I, the less the difference in age at which earnings begin to decline in all schooling groups. If retirement age is related to the time of onset of declining earning power, this analysis might well explain why persons with more schooling retire later in life, and yet have a somewhat shorter earnings span.

So long as gross investment extends over the working life and retirement age is not earlier for the more educated, I_2 is likely to exceed I_1 at each age. This is the simplest interpretation of the universally observed divergence ("fanning out") of *age profiles* of earnings. Note that if I_2 declines more steeply than I_1 (without intersecting), *logarithmic age profiles* will still *diverge* ("fan out"), but *log experience* profiles will *converge:* earnings of higher schooling groups will grow at a somewhat slower rate. *Dollar age profiles* will fan out, a fortiori, and so may[5] dollar experience profiles, even though log experience profiles converge.

A positive correlation between dollar investments in schooling and at work does not constitute evidence against the possibilities for

---

5. A convergence of log experience profiles would mean that the more schooled persons spend less "time" in post-school investment. However, they clearly spend more in dollar terms, if $I_2 > I_1$ at each age. The sufficient condition for a positive correlation between schooling and post-school investments in dollars is even weaker: $C_2 > C_1$ in each year of experience.

substitution between the two forms of investment in human capital. Rather, it reflects the dominance of individual differences in factors determining the scale of total human capital accumulation. Individuals who invest more in human capital, invest more in both forms of it. Evidently, abilities to learn on the job are positively, though far from perfectly, related to abilities to learn at school, and so are financial opportunities to incur such investments. Indeed, given imperfect markets for human capital, it would not be surprising to find that just as schooling investments are positively related to personal (family) income, so are post-school investments to personal earning capacity, that is, to the preceding schooling investments.

As already noted, a positive correlation between dollar schooling and post-school investments does not imply a positive correlation between these investments in "time" units. If individuals with differing amounts of schooling all have the same post-school investment ratios, as indicated by the parallel investment profiles in Figure 2.1, then the correlation between "time" spent in school and in post-school investments is zero. However, *dollar* post-school investments are larger in proportion to the larger earning capacity (initial gross earnings) of the more schooled. This case can be described as one of unitary elasticity of post-school investments with respect to earning capacity. The positive elasticity is less than 1 when dollar post-school investments are larger at higher schooling levels, but less than in proportion to the higher earning capacity.

We may now summarize our conclusions concerning comparative earnings profiles for different schooling groups, and the implications of these comparisons for earnings differentials by schooling, age, and experience. So long as the elasticity (or "marginal propensity to invest") is positive with respect to earning capacity (correlation between dollar schooling and post-school investments is positive), dollar earnings grow faster in upper schooling groups, at given years of experience and — a fortiori — of age. Logarithmic profiles fan out with age, so long as $l_2 > l$, but not necessarily with experience. They converge with experience if the "income elasticity of investment" is less than 1, that is, when the correlation between "time" in schooling and in post-school investment is negative.

Hence "skill differentials" in dollar earnings which are attributable to schooling differences can be expected to grow with age and experience, and relative (percentage) differentials to grow with age.

The latter also grow with experience, but only if the elasticity of post-school investments with respect to earnings capacity exceeds 1. They decline with experience if the elasticity is less than 1, and remain fixed at all stages of experience when the elasticity is 1.

2.3   DISTRIBUTION OF EARNINGS

Thus far I dealt with intergroup differences in earnings of persons differing in schooling and age.

However, within groups of workers of the same schooling and age, earnings inequality is far from negligible. There are several reasons for this: (1) differences in accumulated human capital, despite the same *length* of schooling, because of differences in schooling quality or rates of return to schooling; (2) differences in post-school investment behavior;[6] and (3) differences in rates of return to post-school investments.

2.3.1   VARIANCES

Assume first that individuals who complete a given level of schooling have the same gross earnings (earning capacity) Y_s and rates of return r_j, but differ in their post-school investment behavior.

Individual differences in post-school investments were illustrated in Figure 2.1. The conclusion was that earnings of individuals who invest more in each year j rise more rapidly with experience and for a longer period. This means that relative (as well as absolute) dispersion of *gross earnings* within a schooling cohort rises with experience until peak earnings are reached by the largest investors.

Note, however, that the change in dispersion of *net earnings* with age is not monotonic: Assuming, as I have thus far, that Y_s and r are fixed within schooling groups, earnings of investors are initially smaller than those of noninvestors. Only after the over-taking year of experience $(\hat{j})$ do their earnings surpass those of non-investors. In this case, earnings profiles of individuals with the same schooling but differing in post-school investments will *cross* in the

---

6. Such as job training, job search, or investment in health. Effects of differences in job search behavior have been analyzed by Stigler in his pioneering work on information in labor markets (1962).

neighborhood of $\hat{j}$, reaching the smallest dispersion in that neighborhood. More generally, $\hat{j}$ is not the same for each investor, but it has a strong central tendency, if, in the period preceding $\hat{j}$, the rate of decline of investments, is similar even though its volume differs among investors.

In the special case, where Y_s and $\hat{j}$ are the same for all, dispersion first diminishes, reaching zero at time $\hat{j}$, and increases thereafter. If $\hat{j}$ differs, a minimum but nonzero dispersion is reached at some average $\hat{j}$.

The assumption that initial post-school earning capacities Y_s are the same among persons with the same schooling is not tenable. For the moment, let us keep r the same for these individuals and for all their investments. Let i indicate individual differences in the earnings function:

$$E_{ij} = Y_{si} + r \sum_j C_{ij}.$$

Then,

$$\sigma^2(E_{ij}) = \sigma^2(Y_{si}) + r^2\sigma^2 \left(\sum_j C_{ij}\right) + 2\rho r\sigma(Y_{si})\sigma \left(\sum_j C_{ij}\right), \qquad (2.8)$$

where ρ is the correlation between dollar post-school investments and (dollar) earning capacity. If this correlation is nonnegative, the dollar variance of gross earnings must rise with experience (j), since $\sigma^2(\Sigma_j C_j)$ increases with j. This is because the variance of a sum must increase when the sum is generated by positively correlated increments.

If the positive correlation ρ is not too weak, the monotonic growth in dollar variances will also be observed in *net* earnings,[7] since $\sigma^2(Y_0) = \sigma^2(Y_s - C_0)$, and $\sigma^2(Y_0) < \sigma^2(Y_s)$, so long as $\rho(C_0, Y_s) > \sigma(C_0)/\sigma(Y_s)$. That is, the initial (first-year) variance in net earnings will be smaller than the variance at overtaking, which will, in turn, be smaller than subsequent variances, according to (2.8). The size order of the variances is changed if ρ is small. By the same token, if ρ is negative and sufficiently large, a monotonic decline occurs.

---

7. An example of the effects of such a positive correlation is the growth in the dispersion of earnings due to better recognition of differences in productivity of workers whose initial wages were similar. This may be viewed as worker investment in employer information about their quality. Cf. Stigler (1962).

Exactly the same arithmetic applies to variances of logs. Their profiles depend on the correlation between initial post-school earning capacity (ln Y_{si}) and investment ratios k_i. A strong positive correlation leads to monotonic growth of relative (log) variances with experience, a strong negative correlation produces a monotonic decline, while a weak correlation creates U-shaped experience profiles of log variances. The bottom of the U-shaped profile is found at the overtaking period only when the correlation is zero. Negative correlations shift it to later periods; positive correlations, to earlier periods.

If, as is suggested by Figure 2.1, positive and near-unitary elasticities hold, we would expect to observe dollar variances monotonically increasing with experience but U-shaped profiles of relative variances.

According to the same kind of analysis, the dollar variance of earnings within a schooling group at the "overtaking" stage of experience is larger the higher the schooling level. Since

$$Y_{si} = Y_0 + r \sum_s C_{si},$$

therefore,

$$\sigma^2(Y_{si}) = \sigma^2(Y_0) + r^2\sigma^2 \left(\sum_s C_{si} \right), \tag{2.9}$$

and $\sigma^2(\Sigma_s C_{si})$ grows with increments of schooling. Other things equal, particularly r and the correlation parameter ρ, expression (2.9) implies that dollar variances of earnings increase with level of schooling at each stage of experience.

The relation between relative (log) variances and level of schooling would be the same if similar assumptions could be made about correlations between time-equivalents of investment components. This is not the case, however, as the empirical analysis in Part II indicates.

Thus far I have neglected individual differences in rates of return. Once differences in r_i are assumed, age changes in dispersion can be generated, provided post-school investment is assumed as well, since variations in rates of return alone are not sufficient to generate age changes in the dispersion of earnings. However, it is not necessary in this case to assume that post-school investment differs among persons.

For simplicity, look at gross earnings:

$$E_{ji} = Y_{si} + r_i \sum_j C_{ji}.$$

Assume $\sigma^2(r_i) > 0$, and $C_{ji} = C_j$ for all i. If $C_j = 0$, $\sigma^2(E_{ji})$ remains fixed throughout earning life. But if $C_j > 0$, $\sigma^2(E_{ji})$ increases with j, assuming that r_i and Y_{si} are not negatively correlated:

$$\sigma^2(E_{ji}) = \sigma^2(Y_{si}) + (\Sigma C_j)^2 \sigma^2(r) + 2\rho(\Sigma C_j)\sigma(Y_s)\sigma(r). \qquad (2.10)$$

Note that variances of net earnings are the same as variances of gross earnings when investments are the same for all. A similar monotonic growth of relative variances can be derived from the logarithmic formulation. If reversals or declines in profiles of variances are observed, the hypothesis that post-school investments do not vary among individuals must be rejected. In the logarithmic case the implication is that $\sigma^2(k_i) > 0$. This test is of some importance, because the dispersion in earnings of persons with the same schooling represents an exaggerated index of risk if it is attributed solely to variation in rates of return. A general approach is to assume both $\sigma^2(C_{ij}) > 0$ and $\sigma^2(r_i) > 0$. The empirical implications remain qualitatively the same as when only $\sigma^2(C_{ij}) > 0$.

I conclude that the fanning out of dollar variances and the possible reversals or declines in profiles of relative variances of earnings within schooling groups reflect systematic age increments and individual differences in the scale of human capital investments, rather than random increments ("shocks") in earnings, as the exclusively stochastic theories of income distribution would have it.[8]

Finally, the conclusions about the determinants of earnings dispersion that were expressed for the schooling model by (2.7)[9] can be directly generalized by earnings function (1.4). The logarithmic version is required for studying relative inequality, and a simplified formulation parallel to (2.7), in which correlations among terms are ignored, is derived as follows:

$$\ln E_{ji} = \ln Y_{si} + r_{ji}K_{ji},$$

where

$$K_j = \sum_{t=0}^{j-1} k_t.$$

---

8. See Part II, Table 7.2, for empirical evidence against random shock models.
9. Section A, above.

Then

$$\sigma^2(\ln E_j) = \sigma^2(\ln Y_s) + \bar{r}_j^2\sigma^2(K_j) + \bar{K}_j^2\sigma^2(r_j) + \sigma^2(K_j)\sigma^2(r_j). \quad (2.11)$$

The positive determinants of $\sigma^2(\ln Y_s)$ in (2.7) were initial capacity levels and dispersions in schooling investments s and in rates of return r_s. Now (2.11) adds the corresponding parameters of the distribution of post-school investments as parameters of inequality of gross earnings in an experience group j. Incidentally, the inequality determined in the schooling model, $\sigma^2(\ln Y_{si})$, can be seen, under simplified assumptions, as the inequality in a particular experience group, when $j = \hat{j}$. The overall inequality, however, is of a distribution of earnings of workers who are at different levels of experience in their working life.

2.3.2 AGGREGATION OF VARIANCES

The aggregation of variances of overall years of experience in a schooling group is visualized by the well-known aggregation formula for variances:

$$\sigma_T^2 = \sum \frac{n_j}{n} (\sigma_j^2 + d_j^2), \quad (2.12)$$

where T is an aggregate of several j groups; σ_j^2, the within-group variances; $d_j = \mu_j - \mu_T$, the differences between the means of group j and the overall mean; n_j, the number of observations in j; and n, the total number of observations.

The size of d_j^2 is clearly a positive function of the rate of growth of mean earnings with experience. In dollar terms, therefore, we should expect variances of earnings to increase with length of schooling, if relative frequencies of numbers of workers are similar by years of experience. However, because of upward secular trends in schooling, these frequencies are not similar: there are relatively fewer older workers in the upper schooling groups. Consequently, the increase in dollar variances of earnings with schooling is somewhat attenuated. The conclusions about relative variances of earnings classified by schooling cannot be determined a priori. A discussion of findings based on empirical data is deferred to Part II.

Formula (2.12) is equally applicable to an aggregation of variances over all years of schooling in a given experience group. Because σ_j and d_j in dollar terms increase with experience, increases in the dispersion of earnings by experience and (a fortiori) by age are predictable. Relative variances are not expected to grow monotonically with experience, because reversals are likely to arise some time during the working life. In a classification by age, the growth of relative variances with age is likely to dominate, but reversals may still occur. The attenuation of inequality which is due to secular trends in schooling holds for schooling, experience, and age aggregations, as well as for total inequality observed in the cross section.[10]

2.3.3 SKEWNESS

Positive skewness is a well-known feature of income distributions. Human capital models can explain skewness in several different, not mutually exclusively ways:

a. It will be recalled that the distribution of investment time-equivalents, $h_i = S_i + K_i$, tends to impart positive skewness to the distribution of earnings, even when investments are symmetric. Suppose, therefore, that without investments, the distribution of earnings Y_0 would be symmetric. In that case, the distribution of ln Y_0 would be negatively skewed and so would the distribution of ln Y_i, given a symmetric distribution of investments. Thus, unless the distribution of investments has a strong positive skew, the *logarithmic* distribution of earnings will be negatively skewed. At the same time, unless the distribution of investments has a substantial negative skew, the distribution of *dollar* earnings will be positively skewed. *A normal distribution of "raw abilities" is, therefore, likely to produce a positively skewed distribution of earnings with a shape intermediate between normal and log normal.* The larger the investment component $r(S + K)$ in earnings, the better the log normal rather than normal approximation.

b. Assume that the distribution of r_i is symmetric, and ignore variation in Y_{0i}. In that case, even for fixed h, the distribution of earnings would be positively skewed. As before, positive skewness would be accentuated at higher levels of investment h.

---

10. To state that inequality in the cross section is, in part, affected by the rate of change of secular trends in schooling is to ignore possible feedbacks of such trends on rates of return. Such effects depend on the nature of the trends, a subject outside the scope of this study.

c. An important conclusion emerges from the analysis of within-group variances: systematic allocations of individuals' investments in human capital over their life cycle and systematic differences among individuals in the scale of their investments show up as positive correlations among instalments of investment within and between the schooling and post-school stage. Consequently, dollar variances of earnings are positively related to experience (age within schooling groups) and to schooling (at given years of experience). Since average earnings must grow with schooling and experience, the allocation of human capital investments produces a positive correlation between means and variances across subgroups of workers defined by schooling and experience. The positive correlation between means and variances of subsets of the distribution leads to positive skewness in the aggregate. This explanation of skewness is additional and independent of assumptions about the shape of the distribution of schooling which were emphasized in the schooling model.[11] It is the only explanation inherent in the human capital model of individual behavior.

The conclusions about positive skewness in the aggregate do not apply to the logarithms of earnings, because, as the previous discussion suggested, log earnings are likely to be negatively skewed within groups, and an a-priori case for a positive correlation between logarithmic means and variances in subgroups is not clear.[12]

The effects of secular trends in schooling on the distribution of earnings is an important example of the distinction between observations in cohorts and in cross sections. Though the theoretical analysis is carried out in longitudinal (cohort) terms, empirical analysis and interest focus on the distribution of earnings in a cross section in a given period of time. The possible considerations impinging on this distinction are too numerous for a useful a-priori analysis, given the limited information available. However, the distinction between cohorts and cross sections receives attention, where possible and appropriate, in the empirical analysis of Part II, below.

---

11. See the mathematical note at the end of this chapter.

12. Both in dollars and in logs, aggregate skewness in the cross section is also affected by secular trends in schooling in a manner analogous to the effects on variances, as discussed above.

2.4 MATHEMATICAL NOTE ON SKEWNESS

Let

N = population of an aggregate; M, its mean; σ, its standard deviation; and α, its third moment (skewness).

n_i = population of component i; M_i, its mean; σ_i, its standard deviation; and α_i, its skewness.

$d_i = M_i - M$.

Then [13]

$$\alpha = \frac{\Sigma_i n_i \sigma_i^3 \alpha_i + \Sigma_i n_i d_i (3\sigma_i^2 + d_i^2)}{N\sigma^3}. \tag{2.13}$$

With the help of this relation we can (1) investigate the conditions under which a combination of symmetric distributions of the components results in a positively skewed aggregate, (2) show that the theoretical model ensures such a result.

Let $\alpha_i = 0$, hence

$$\alpha = \frac{\Sigma_i n_i d_i (3\sigma_i^2 + d_i^2)}{N\sigma^3}$$

$$= \frac{\Sigma_i n_i d_i^3 + \Sigma_i 3 n_i d_i \sigma_i^2}{N\sigma^3}. \tag{2.14}$$

Since the denominator is positive, aggregative skewness will be positive ($\alpha > 0$), if and only if:

$$\Sigma_i n_i d_i^3 + \Sigma_i 3 n_i d_i \sigma_i^2 > 0.$$

A. If no intragroup dispersion exists ($\sigma_i = 0$), or if all component dispersions are the same ($\sigma_i = C$), the second term vanishes:

$$\Sigma_i 3 n_i d_i \sigma_i^2 = 3C\Sigma_i n_i (M_i - M) = 3C(NM - NM) = 0.$$

In this case aggregate skewness is positive, if and only if

$$\Sigma_i n_i d_i^3 > 0. \tag{2.15}$$

This expression is, in fact, the third moment in the distribution of component means around the aggregate mean. When the i's are interpreted as schooling groups, expression (2.15) measures skew-

---

13. For derivation, see Bates (1935, pp. 95–98).

ness introduced by the distribution of schooling alone. In the school-ing model this is positive, provided the skewness of the schooling distribution is not excessively negative.

B. If intragroup dispersion does exist ($\sigma_i > 0$), and differs from group to group, the factor $3\Sigma_i n_i d_i \sigma_i^2$ can be interpreted as the contribution of intragroup differentials to aggregate skewness. The condition for

$$\Sigma_i 3 n_i d_i \sigma_i^2 > 0 \tag{2.16}$$

is

$$\Sigma_i n_i M_i \sigma_i^2 > \Sigma_i n_i M \sigma_i^2.$$

Dividing both sides of the inequality by $\Sigma_i n_i M_i = NM$ we get:

$$\frac{\Sigma_i n_i M_i \sigma_i^2}{\Sigma_i n_i M_i} > \frac{\Sigma_i n_i \sigma_i^2}{\Sigma_i n_i}. \tag{2.17}$$

In other words, in order for (2.16) to hold, the weighted average of the intragroup variances weighted by $n_i M_i$ must exceed the average of these variances weighted by n_i. Clearly, this occurs when the σ_i^2's are positively correlated with the M_i's. This condition holds in the complete model, in which intragroup dispersion is expected to increase with the average accumulated investment $(S + K)$, hence with average earnings.

Part II

EMPIRICAL ANALYSIS

3

Schooling and Earnings

3.1 QUANTITATIVE ANALYSIS

Human capital models have been employed in empirical analyses of income distributions in attempts to explain differences in level, inequality, and skewness of earnings of workers who differ by schooling and age, to interpret shapes of age-earnings profiles of individuals, and to explain differences in earnings distributions among regions and countries.[1] Though sketchy in many respects, these studies tend to provide at least qualitatively consistent interpretations of some of the apparently bewildering variety of features of income distributions.

There is as yet no evidence of quantitative explanatory power of the human capital model to match the promise indicated by the qualitative or comparative analyses. As yet, no serious attempts have been made at a full quantitative accounting of the effects of the distribution of investment in human capital on observed earnings inequality. The only available empirical estimates of the extent of in-

---

1. Mincer (1957, 1958, 1962), Becker (1964, 1967), Ben-Porath (1967), Chiswick (1967), Lydall (1968).

come inequality[2] that can be attributed to investments in human capital are limited to investments in schooling, measured by years of schooling.

Applying the "schooling model" (equation 1.3) in a simple regression of 1959 log earnings of men aged 25–64 in the experienced labor force on their years of schooling, Chiswick found coefficients of determination varying between 10–20 per cent within U.S. regions and states. The coefficients are 10 per cent and 18 per cent for earnings of white men in the non-South and South, respectively. Within states, Chiswick applied regressions to incomes of men aged 25 and over, instead of earnings, which were not available in the published 1960 Census data.

Low as they are, the coefficients of determination are overstated, because they are based on data grouped by income and schooling intervals. Application of the same regression to individual observations of 1959 earnings of all U.S. white, nonfarm, nonstudent males,[3] aged 15–64 yields a coefficient of determination of barely 7 per cent.

The inadequacy of the schooling model as an explanation of inequality, which is measured here by the variance of log earnings, is apparent not only in the low coefficients of determination but also in the small slope coefficients of the regression. According to equation (1.3) these coefficients are supposed to represent estimates of average rates of return on investments in schooling. But as Chiswick's data and my Table 4.4, below (first row) show, the regression slopes are substantially lower, almost half the size of internal rates calculated directly from age profiles by Becker, Hansen, and Hanoch.

The disappointing performance of the schooling model need not cast doubt on the relevance or importance of human capital analysis. As the discussion in Part I indicates, the schooling model represents an incomplete specification of human capital theory of the distribution of earnings. The model cannot adequately explain in-

---

2. Though the human capital model applies strictly to labor incomes, the empirical literature often describes total incomes rather than earnings.

3. These were males with some earnings in 1959. Earnings were defined as wages and salaries plus self-employment income, provided wages and salaries were the major source of earnings. The 1/1,000 sample of the 1960 U.S. population Census, used in this study, contained 31,093 men in this category. The earnings of over 95 per cent of them consisted of wages and salaries alone. This is the basic body of data used in our empirical analyses.

equality of earnings among individuals who differ not only in schooling but also in other behavioral characteristics including, in particular, other forms of investments in human capital. In the empirical analyses that follow, it will be seen that when the human capital model is expanded to include post-school investments its explanatory power is greatly increased. In the expanded model biases in the regression estimates of the schooling model are removed. Although the inclusion of an undifferentiated and indirect concept of post-school investments constitutes only an initial step toward a more complete analysis, it provides a unified interpretation for a variety of qualitative and quantitative aspects of the structure of earnings.

3.1.1 GROUPED DATA

Before proceeding to incorporate post-school investment behavior into the empirical analysis, it is useful to consider the applicability of the schooling model somewhat more closely. As we have seen, the schooling model is too blunt an instrument for analyzing the ungrouped distribution of earnings. Evidently, variation in earnings within schooling groups is a major part of total inequality. With grouped data, the positive relation between schooling and earnings does, of course, emerge clearly. Still, the model does not fit properly in one respect: The slope of line 1, Chart 3.1, that is, the regression slope of average earnings (in logs) on years of schooling, is again too flat, as it was in the ungrouped regression. Apparently, grouping does does not eliminate the problem of within-group variation of earnings. These earnings have been averaged in each schooling group, but the average depends on the age distribution in the groups, given the existence of pronounced age-earnings profiles. As is well known, earnings at later stages of work experience are substantially higher than at early stages. Because of strong secular trends in schooling, average age is older in the lower schooling groups, younger in the higher schooling groups (Table 3.1, column 2, below). Consequently, earnings differentials among schooling groups, shown as the slope of line 1, Chart 3.1, are understated. But, even if earnings of a fixed age group (e.g., age 32–33, line 2, Chart 3.1) are compared, the downward bias in the slope is still not removed.

The basic reason for the persistent bias becomes intuitively apparent if it is assumed that the individual growth curve of earnings is

CHART 3.1
SCHOOLING AND AVERAGE EARNINGS, 1959
(schooling groups of white, nonfarm men)

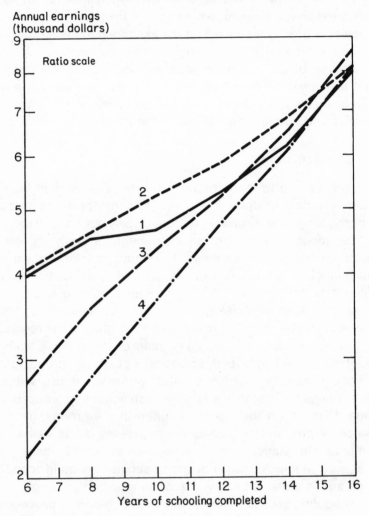

NOTE:
Curve *1:* average earnings of all workers, age 15–64.
Curve *2:* average earnings at age 32–33.
Curve *3:* average earnings with 10 years of experience.
Curve *4:* average earnings with 7–9 years of experience.
SOURCE: 1/1,000 sample of U.S. Census, 1960. Estimates are shown in Table 3.1.

largely a function of post-school investment, such as on-the-job and other forms of training and experience. The earnings profile is a function of work experience rather than of age: Since less schooled persons enter the labor force earlier, they spend more time acquiring work experience; at a given age, they will reach higher relative levels of their earnings profiles than persons of the same age, but with more schooling. This is why earnings differentials are still understated in line 2. On this post-school investment hypothesis, the more appropriate standardization is for years of experience rather than age. Empirical support for the argument is found in line 3 of Chart 3.1, where earnings are shown at ages corresponding to a decade after completion of schooling. The slope of line 3 is almost double that of lines 1 and 2, and is indeed well within the usual range of directly calculated internal rates of return (about 12 per cent).

In the absence of direct information in the 1960 Census, years of work experience were measured by subtracting the age of completion of schooling from reported age. Average ages of school leaving were estimated by Hanoch (1968) from the same data (cf. Table 3.1, column 2). Conceptually, age is not irrelevant, since it is a factor in the depreciation of human capital stock. Separate estimates of age and experience effects on earnings require individual data on job experience. Such estimates as are available indicate that experience, rather than age, is the dominant factor in earnings.[4]

The intuitive argument in support of a standardization by years of experience does not indicate the particular stage of experience at which earnings of different schooling groups should be compared. But the decade of experience chosen for line 3 is not entirely arbitrary. The argument and evidence can be more rigorously stated, paying closer attention to the concepts implicit in the schooling model (1.3):

$$\ln Y_s = \ln Y_0 + rs.$$

Implementation of this model is a problem not only because the variation in earnings within schooling groups is omitted, but also because data for the (dependent) earnings variable are not available. According to the derivation of the schooling models, Y_s represents a hypothetical concept of earnings a person would receive after completion of schooling, if he did not incur any further growth-producing

---

4. See discussion in Chapter 4, below.

TABLE 3.1

SCHOOLING, AVERAGE ANNUAL EARNINGS, AND RATES OF RETURN, 1959
(U.S. white, nonfarm men)

| Years of Schooling (1) | Me-dian Age (2) | Age at First Year of Ex-peri-ence (3) | Average Annual Earnings | | | At Overtaking | | Rate of Return | |
			All Ages (4)	At Age 32–34 (5)	In 10th Year of Experi-ence (6)	Earn-ings (Y_s) (7)	Year (8)	Used (r) (9)	Im-plicit (r_s) (10)
0–4	52	14	$3,350	$3,390	$ 2,520	$1,910	7		
5–7	48	14	4,000	4,070	2,740	2,130	7	(17)	
8	45	16	4,520	4,600	3,580	2,830	7	16	19.6
9–11	36	18	4,660	5,250	4,360	3,660	7–8	(14)	
12	34	20	5,330	5,870	5,280	4,800	8	13	13.2
13–15	33	23	6,240	6,850	6,520	6,100	8–9	(11)	
16	35	25	8,020	8,160	8,600	7,950	8–9	10	10.1
17+	37	28	9,200	8,710	10,200	9,900	9	(9)	7.3

NOTE:

Col. 3:   Estimates of Hanoch (1967): Mean age at the terminal school year plus
1. These estimates were modified in the lowest two groups by the assumption that boys did not enter the labor force before the age of
fourteen. Also, an average of five rather than six years was estimated
as the average duration of college studies.

Cols. 4–7: 1/1,000 sample of U.S. Census, 1960.

Cols. 7–8: Uses estimate of r in column 9 to equate the present values of Y_s in
column 7 with the present values of the observed profiles.

Col. 9:   Values in parentheses are extrapolated.

Col. 10: $r_s = (\ln Y_{s_2} - \ln Y_{s_1})/\Delta s$.

self-investments. Values of Y_s are not observable, but as was shown
in Chapter 1, they can be approximated if certain assumptions are
accepted.

The two basic assumptions are that rates of return to schooling
are not very different from rates of return to post-school investment,
and that earnings profiles Y_s with no further (net) investment remain
largely flat for most of the working life. Both assumptions are empirical, and some evidence in their support is considered in later
discussion.

Recall the expanded earnings function (1.4):

$$Y_{s_{ij}} = Y_{si} + (r \sum_{t=0}^{j-1} C_{ti} - C_{ji}),$$

Here Y_{sij} denotes net earnings of person i with s years of schooling who is in his jth year of work experience; C_j, dollar costs of post-school investments; and r, rates of return to post-school investments. Since the first expression on the right is Y_{si}, gross earnings after completion of schooling, it equals the observed earnings Y_{sij} at the stage of experience $j = \hat{j}$, when the second right-hand term is equal to zero.
As was demonstrated in equation (1.10), $\hat{j} < 1/r$. If r is not very different from the rates of return as usually calculated, the "overtaking" year of experience at which observed earnings $Y_{sij} = E_s$ should be a decade or less. As a rough guess, earnings at ten years after completion of schooling were used in line 3 of Chart 3.1.

A more direct approach is to estimate Y_s as that amount of annual earnings in a constant income stream whose present value equals the present value of the actual earnings profile. The present values must be taken at the start of working life, and the rate of return is used as the rate of discount. Such estimates of earnings Y_s are utilized in line 4 of Chart 3.1. Its slope is somewhat steeper than that of line 3, because higher rates of return, hence earlier "overtaking" years of experience and lower earnings than in line 3, were assigned to the lower schooling groups.[5] The overtaking years of experience run from 7 in the lower to 9 in the higher schooling groups.

The earnings figures (Y_s), the estimated years at overtaking ($\hat{j}$), internal rates (r) used for estimating them,[6] and the slopes of the lines (r_s), are shown in Table 3.1 (columns 7, 8, 9, and 10, respectively). Note that the slope r_s in the schooling model (1.3) is an estimate of the rate of return to schooling only, while the rate as usually calculated (r) from age profiles, although often called a rate of return to education or schooling, is a rate on a mix of schooling and post-

---

5. The causes of the differences in slopes of the four lines in Chart 3.1 are perhaps best visualized by inspection of Chart 4.3 in Chapter 4, which shows the age profiles of log earnings in the several schooling groups. The slope of line 1 corresponds to the vertical distance (per school year) between points at mean ages; the slope of line 2 corresponds to the distance ABC at age 33; while the slopes of lines 3 and 4 correspond to the distances between the estimated overtaking points ($A^1B^1C^1$). The last is the best estimate. It is necessarily the steepest.

6. These rates were calculated from the earnings profiles shown in Charts 4.1 and 4.2. Direct costs and student earnings were conveniently ignored in the calculation, on the assumption of their rough cancellation at higher levels and unimportance at lower levels. In this I follow Hanoch (1968). The assumption is not tenable in general, but rough estimates suffice for the present analysis.

TABLE 3.2
SHORT-CUT AND STANDARD ESTIMATES OF RATES OF RETURN [a]
TO SCHOOLING, 1939, 1949, 1958
(U.S. white, nonfarm men)

| | High School | | College [b] | |
| | Short Cut | Standard | Short Cut | Standard |
Year	(1)	(2)	(1)	(2)
1939	15.1%	12.5%	12.8%	11.0%
1949	13.5	11.8	10.6	10.6
1958	14.4	15.1	10.2	11.5

SOURCE: Mincer (1962).
a. For 1939, data are based on earnings; for 1949 and 1958, based on income.
b. For 1939 and 1949, refers to persons having more than sixteen years of schooling; for 1958, sixteen years.

school investment. It is a weighted average of the rates on schooling (r_s) and on post-school investments (r_p).[7] In constructing lines *3* and *4* of Chart 3.1, it was assumed that r_s and r, hence r_s and r_p, do not differ. A rough check of consistency appears in the results in Table 3.1. A comparison of r_s estimated by the slopes of line *4* and of the *r* utilized for its construction shows them to be very close at the college and high school levels (Table 3.1, columns 9 and 10). The small discrepancy at these levels suggests that it is not misleading to label internal rates of return calculated from earnings profiles as "rates of return to education." Lines *3* and *4* are not only steeper, but also straighter than line *1*. Evidently, the closer the correspondence of the data to the concepts of the model, the better the empirical fit.[8] Actually, linearity is not required by the model, since *r* may differ by level of schooling. Nonetheless, the broken shape of line *1* is more likely to reflect a bad fit than erratically different values of *r*.

The experiments reported above indicate that although the schooling model is incomplete, it is relevant to the analysis of

---

7. Cf. Becker (1964, p. 42).

8. Lydall (1959) attempted to test the "goodness of fit" of the semilog form of the schooling model, using line *1*. This, as we have seen, is not the most appropriate test. Nevertheless, he would not have rejected the model had he not mistakenly used a double-log form in his test (p. 95).

earnings differentials. Moreover, its proper empirical implementation gives rise to a useful by-product: a quick and easy, though rough, method of assessing rates of return to *schooling*. Data for fewer than the first ten years of earnings are needed for the purpose, a major advantage in up-to-date analysis, compared to procedures which require information on a whole working life of earnings.

Table 3.2, column 1, shows estimates of rates of return to *schooling* calculated by assigning ages 23, 28, and 33–34 as the periods of overtaking to elementary school, high school, and college graduates. The ages are taken from Table 3.1 (column 3 + column 8). This calculation, the same as in column 10 of Table 3.1, utilizes only one earnings figure in each schooling group. In contrast, the rates of return shown in column 2 of Table 3.2 were calculated from complete age profiles of earnings. The similarity is rather close, a strong suggestion of the feasibility of "short-cut" estimation.

3.1.2 UNGROUPED DATA

The schooling model will now be explored in ungrouped, individual data. Overtaking values of earnings Y_s which were estimated for schooling groups can also be estimated, under somewhat stronger assumptions, for individuals whose schooling is known. Since, at $\hat{j}$,

$$r_p = C_{\hat{j}} \Big/ \sum_{t=0}^{j-1} C_t,$$

if all individuals in a schooling group are assumed to have the same rate of return to, and proportionate time distribution of, post-school investments, the overtaking year of experience $(\hat{j})$ would be the same for all. On this assumption we may select a set of individuals in our sample whose years of work experience correspond to the overtaking years which were used in the grouped data. The distribution of earnings of these individuals can be viewed as an estimate of the latent distribution of earnings that would be received if no further human capital were invested after completion of schooling.

As indicated in Table 3.3, below, I selected several subsets of the sample to approximate the distribution of earnings at overtaking. The findings in Table 3.3 do not vary much among the samples. As expected, earnings inequality in the overtaking sets is smaller than aggregate inequality. Indeed, the earnings at this stage of the life cycle are an estimate of lifetime earnings, since the present value of Y_s approximates the present value of the observed earnings profile. The variance of log earnings in this group is about 0.50 (Table 3.3, column 6) compared to 0.68 in the aggregate. Thus, at the start of working life, expected lifetime inequality measured in relative terms (in logs), is about 25 per cent less than aggregate inequality. The difference in dollar dispersions is greater. The dollar variance of the aggregate cross-sectional distribution of annual earnings is about twice the size of the dollar dispersion in the overtaking set.

The earnings distribution at overtaking serves two purposes: As suggested above, it provides a base for assessing the contribution of post-school investments to aggregate inequality. More directly, it serves as a testing ground for the schooling model, since the latter can be directly applied only to earnings of this particular population group. However, for several reasons, the inequality estimated in the overtaking set cannot be fully explained by differences in *years* of schooling alone:

a. The distribution of schooling investments is only partly measured by the distribution of *years* of schooling. The dispersion in years of schooling fails to reflect variation in initial earning capacity and in expenditures of time and money of students attending schools of the same quality, as well as schools of differing quality.[9]

b. The empirical definition of the "overtaking" set is quite rough. In the absence of specific information each individual was assigned the average age of school-leaving in his schooling group. Actual dispersion in those ages is not negligible.[10]

c. Overtaking years differ among people with the same amount of schooling and experience, if their rates of return differ, and if their dollar investment profiles are not proportional. The observed residual variances in the regressions of (log) earnings on years of schooling in the empirical overtaking sets, as presented in Table 3.3, column 5, must, therefore, overstate the true residual variation.

---

9. Information on direct costs and earnings of students can be incorporated into the calculation of investment ratios k during school years, instead of assuming that each $k = 1$.

10. National Science Foundation data for 1966 from the National Register of Scientific and Technical Personnel indicate standard deviations of 2 to 3 years for ages at which B.A. and higher degrees were obtained (Weiss, 1971).

TABLE 3.3
Regressions in Overtaking Sets

Years of Experience (1)	Number of Observations (2)	Regression Equation (3)	R^2 (4)	$\sigma^2(u)$ (5)	$\sigma^2(\ln Y)$ (6)	$\sigma(r)$ (7)
8	790	(1) $\ln Y = 6.36 + .162s$ (16.4)	.306	.333	.48	.046
	$\bar{s} = 12.1$ $\sigma^2(s) = 7.4$	(2) $\ln Y = 2.14 + .115s + 1.27 \ln W$ (15.1) (21.0)	.575	.204		.036
6–10	3,689	(1) $\ln Y = 6.75 + .133s$ (36.1)	.261	.422	.56	.052
	$\bar{s} = 12.2$ $\sigma^2(s) = 7.9$	(2) $\ln Y = 2.07 + .104s + 1.31 \ln W$ (34.0) (43.4)	.511	.279		.042
7–9	2,124	(1) $\ln Y = 6.30 + .165s$ (26.5)	.328	.353	.52	.048
	$\bar{s} = 12.2$ $\sigma^2(s) = 7.7$	(2) $\ln Y = 1.89 + .121s + 1.29 \ln W$ (24.6) (30.6)	.596	.218		.037
		(3) $\ln Y = 4.78 + .424s - .010s^2$ (10.0) (−6.1)	.347			
		(4) $\ln Y = 1.60 + .183s - .002s^2$ (5.3) (−1.7) $+ 1.270 \ln W$ (29.7)	.602	.215		

Note: Figures in parentheses are t ratios; Y = earnings in 1959 of white nonfarm men; s = years of schooling; $\sigma^2(s)$ = variance of years of schooling; W = weeks worked in 1959; R^2 = coefficient of determination; $\sigma^2(u)$ = residual variance; $\sigma^2(\ln Y)$ = aggregate variance; $\sigma(r)$ = standard deviation of rates of return.
Source: 1/1,000 sample of U.S. Census, 1960.

Regressions were run in several alternative subsets of the sample, representing approximations to the overtaking stage of experience. Experiments were carried out with subgroups of different sizes, running from 790 in a single experience year ($j = 8$) to 3,689 individuals in an aggregated (6–10) year-group. The coefficients of determination (R^2) and the regression slopes differ somewhat depending on which interval of experience is chosen. The R^2 in these regressions run from 0.26 to 0.33, while the slopes of the schooling

variable, which are estimates of the (average) rate of return to schooling, vary between 0.13 and 0.16.

Table 3.3 contains results for three subgroups varying in level of
aggregation, but centering around $j = 8$. The regression slopes in
Table 3.3 are estimates of rates of return to schooling. The size of the
slope is affected by the number of weeks worked during the year.
When the regression is expanded to include the number of weeks
(in logs) worked during 1959 (W) as a second variable, the partial
coefficients of schooling (at s) are several percentage points lower
than were the simple coefficients. This is because (logs of) W are
positively correlated with schooling: on the average, longer-schooled
individuals work more weeks during the year. The coefficients for W
are above unity, implying a positive correlation between weekly
earnings and weeks worked during the year even for workers with the
same schooling attainment.

If the positive correlation between weeks worked and schooling
and between weeks worked and weekly earnings reflected primarily
a positively sloped labor supply curve, then the coefficient at s based
on weekly earnings would be the more appropriate estimate of rates
of return to schooling. These correlations may be, however, a consequence of a greater incidence of turnover, unemployment, seasonal-
ity, and illness at lower levels of schooling and earnings. In that case
coefficients at s based on annual earnings would be the more appropriate estimates, if the reduction of such incidence is an effect of
schooling.[11]

Estimates of rates of return directly calculated from age profiles
of earnings (such as those of Becker, Hansen, and Hanoch) are
usually higher at lower levels of schooling. A statistical test of this
inverse relation between r and s is performed in regressions (3) and
(4) in Table 3.3. A quadratic term in s is added to the regression to
allow for a systematic change in r with changing levels of s. A significant negative coefficient at s^2 means that rates of return are lower at
higher levels of schooling. This is, indeed, the case in regression (3).
However, the same test performed in regression (4), where weeks
worked are included, yields a negative sign but a small and statistically insignificant coefficient at the quadratic term. It appears,
therefore, that differences in the amount of time worked during the

---

11. For further discussion of the working-time variable, see Chapter 7, below.

year almost fully account for the higher rates of return at the lower levels of schooling.

A comparison of regressions (2) and (3) suggests that about half of the rate of return to elementary school graduates can be attributed to their greater amount of employment during the year compared to people with less schooling. The employment factor accounts for about a third of the rate of return at the high school level, and is of little importance at the college level: From quadratic regression (3) estimates of marginal r_s are:

$$\frac{d(\ln Y)}{ds} = .424 - .021s.$$

$$\text{For } s = 8, \, r_s = .256$$
$$s = 12, \, r_s = .172$$
$$s = 16, \, r_s = .088$$

The explanatory power of schooling investments in the distribution of earnings at overtaking is underestimated by the regressions of Table 3.3. Variations in quality of schooling and in ages of school-leaving are left in the residual. The latter may account [12] for 0.01 to 0.04 in $\sigma^2(u)$, but the former is likely to be more important. According to figures quoted by Becker (1964, p. 108) the coefficient of variation in expenditures on a college education in New York State alone was no less than the coefficient of variation in the national distribution of years of schooling. Solmon and Wachtel (1972) adjusted years of schooling for "quality" by expressing expenditures per student as a ratio to estimated student opportunity costs and adding these time-equivalents to each student's reported years of schooling. For students with at least a college education in the NBER-Thorndike sample,[13] the variance in the "quality-adjusted" years of schooling was three times the size of the variance of unadjusted years of schooling. According to the same data the dispersion in high school quality was smaller, but still quite considerable. At any rate, a conservative guess would be that the "quality-adjusted" variance of schooling at all levels exceeds the unadjusted variance by a third. If so, R^2 corrected for schooling quality could increase from the ob-

---

12. If the standard deviation of ages at school-leaving is 1 to 2 years within schooling groups (judging by data of Weiss, 1971).

13. For a description of NBER-TH, see Juster (1972).

served 33 per cent to over 40 per cent in the regressions which do not include the weeks-worked variable, and from the observed 60 per cent to perhaps 70 per cent in those that do include it.

Variation in rates of return, which cannot be observed, is probably the main component of residual variation in these regressions. The correlation between these rates and the quantity of schooling investment across individuals is evidently weak, as experiments with the inclusion of s^2 in the regressions (Table 3.3) suggested. If so, the assumption of independence between r_i and s_i across individuals can be used and provides a way of estimating upper limits for the dispersion of individual rates of return $\sigma^2(r)$. In this case the schooling model, equation (1.3), in variance form is:

$$\sigma^2(\ln Y_s) = \bar{r}^2\sigma^2(s) + \bar{s}^2\sigma^2(r) + \sigma^2(s)\sigma^2(r) + \sigma^2(v), \qquad (3.1)$$

where v is a residual due to other unmeasured factors. The residual variance in the regressions of Table 3.3 is:

$$\sigma^2(u) = \bar{s}^2\sigma^2(r) + \sigma^2(s)\sigma^2(r) + \sigma^2(v), \qquad (3.2)$$

with $\sigma^2(v)$ larger in regressions (1) than (2), since the effects of weeks worked are in the residuals of (1). Therefore,

$$\sigma^2(r) < \frac{\sigma^2(u)}{\bar{s}^2 + \sigma^2(s)}. \qquad (3.3)$$

The values of the upper limit for $\sigma(r)$ are shown in column 7 of Table 3.3. They range from 4 per cent in the regressions which are standardized for weeks worked to 5 per cent in those that are not. The coefficient of variation in individual average rates of return is therefore at most a third in each of the regressions.

It is difficult to judge whether the estimated (upper limit) coefficient of variation is "small" or "large." It is apparently much smaller than the coefficient of variation in corporate rates of return, observed by Stigler (1963) in annual data (1947–54).[14] It should be noted that the dispersion of rates of return to schooling is not a good measure of risk to the extent that abilities and opportunities underlying this dispersion are known to the individual.

---

14. Note also that year-to-year instability is far greater in business incomes than in earnings of male adults: The interyear correlations in corporate earnings decay rapidly over time (Stigler, p. 71) in contrast to the slow decline in panel correlations of individual earnings shown in Table 7.1, below.

TABLE 3.4
CORRELATION OF LOG EARNINGS WITH SCHOOLING
WITHIN EXPERIENCE OR AGE GROUPS

Years of Experience	Coeff. of Det. (r^2)		Years of Age	Coeff. of Det. (r^2)
	All [a] (1)	Year-round (2)		(3)
1–3	.31	.25		
4–6	.30	.27	20–24	.02
7–9	.33	.30	25–29	.04
10–12	.26	.30	30–34	.11
13–15	.20	.25	35–39	.14
16–18	.17	.20	40–44	.16
19–21	.16	.18	45–49	.12
22–24	.13	.17	50–54	.12
25–27	.13	.15	55–60	.09
28–30	.12	.14	60–64	.08
31–33	.07	.14		
34–36	.05	.07		
37–39	.07	.09		
Aggregate	.07	.08	Aggregate	.07

SOURCE: 1/1,000 sample of the U.S. Census, 1960.
a. All workers, including both year-round and those whose work was part time, seasonal, or otherwise intermittent.

Without standardization for weeks worked and without adjustment for quality, the schooling model explains a third of the inequality of earnings in the overtaking subset of the earnings distribution. This is a great deal more than the 7 per cent found in the simple regression of log earnings on schooling in the aggregate distribution. The greater applicability of the schooling model to the overtaking period than to subsequent stages of experience is shown clearly in Table 3.4.

As measured by simple coefficients of determination, the effects of schooling on earnings decay continuously in successive three-year experience groups after the first decade of experience. This is shown in columns 1 and 2 of Table 3.4.

The decay of the coefficient of determination (R^2) reflects the growing importance of accumulated experience in the determination of earnings. R^2 is the ratio of "explained" to total variance of log earnings. In the overtaking set

$$R_j^2 = \frac{r^2\sigma^2(s)}{r^2\sigma^2(s) + \sigma^2(u)}. \tag{3.4}$$

The content of the residual variance $\sigma^2(u)$ was already discussed. At later stages when $j > \hat{j}$, assuming little or no correlation between time-equivalents of schooling and post-school investments:

$$R_j^2 = \frac{r^2\sigma^2(s)}{r^2\sigma^2(s) + \sigma^2(u) + \sigma^2(r\sum_{t}^{j-1} k_t - k_j)}. \tag{3.5}$$

R_j^2 declines because the denominator grows with experience, since the right-hand term in it must grow. The decline in R_j^2 may be strengthened for additional reasons: The coefficient of schooling (r) may decline over time—a possibility suggested by a "vintage" hypothesis of schooling effectiveness.[15] A random shock structure in the residual u would give rise to a growing $\sigma^2(u)$, thereby increasing the rate of decay in R^2.

The systematic effects of accumulated experience are obscured when the schooling model is applied to age groups (Table 3.4, column 3): The coefficient of determination at its highest is half the size of that found in the overtaking group.[16] Its peak is reached in the 40–44 age group, and it is quite small before age 30. The weaker fit of the schooling model in age groups compared to experience groups is due to the negative correlation between schooling and post-school investments at given ages. This is most pronounced at the early post-school ages, when investment in experience is heaviest. The later decay is due to the accumulation of post-school investments, as already discussed.

During the first decade of experience, the coefficients of determination are relatively high but somewhat less than at overtaking. It is plausible though not necessary that the denominator in the expres-

---

15. Welch (1972) observes declines in regression coefficients of schooling over experience in both 1960 Census data and 1967 data of the U.S. Department of Labor Survey of Economic Opportunity, and interprets them as "vintage" effects.

16. The contrast is somewhat overstated, as the age intervals are wider.

sion for R^2 decline during the first decade, as suggested in the discussion in Chapter 2.

In a longitudinal study of over 1,500 men who were 30–39 years old in 1968, Blum (1971) also found that the correlation between schooling and earnings was higher after ten years of work experience ($R^2 = .24$) than in the initial year ($R^2 = .16$). Differential post-school investments of individuals can account for the difference.[17]

3.2 SOME QUALITATIVE IMPLICATIONS

When applied to the proper data, the schooling model can be a useful tool for quantitative analysis. More generally, though less rigorously, the model also yields several important qualitative implications about distributions of earnings.

1. A tendency toward positive skewness of earnings is produced by the transformation of absolute differences in years of schooling into relative differentials in earnings. Clearly, by equation (1.3) a symmetric distribution of years of schooling implies a positively skewed distribution of earnings. Unless the skew in the distribution of schooling is highly negative, a positive skew will be imparted to the distribution of earnings. Because of the finite lower limit (zero, or a legal minimum) empirical schooling distributions are more likely to be positively skewed when the average level of schooling is low. Skewness may change from positive to negative as the average level of schooling reaches high levels. Thus the U.S. distribution of schooling has become negatively skewed in the cohorts below age 40, as shown in Table 3.5. Even so, negative skewness in schooling is not sufficient to create negative skewness in earnings. It will be recalled (Chapter 2, note 1) that, according to the schooling model, positive skewness in earnings obtains so long as $1 - (d_2/d_1) < rd_1$, where d_1 is the schooling interval (in years) between the median and a lower (say tenth) percentile and d_2 is the interval between the median and a corresponding upper (ninetieth) percentile. Given rates of return r in excess of 10 per cent, the above condition is empirically satisfied in Table 3.5 in all age groups. A fortiori (cf. section 2.4), the aggregate

---

17. The notion that schooling has a positive effect on earnings merely as a "credential" is difficult to reconcile with the pattern of correlations observed in Table 3.4 and in the longitudinal study.

EMPIRICAL ANALYSIS

TABLE 3.5
DISTRIBUTION OF YEARS OF SCHOOLING (s), BY AGE GROUPS, 1959
(U.S. white, nonfarm males)

Age	P_{10} (1)	Md (2)	P_{90} (3)	$\bar{s}$ (4)	σ_s (5)	$d_u - d_1$ (6)
14–19	6.0	9.8	11.8	10.5	2.2	−1.8
20–24	8.1	11.9	15.2	12.1	2.8	−0.5
25–29	6.8	12.0	16.0	12.2	3.2	−1.2
30–34	6.4	11.8	16.0	11.7	3.4	−1.2
35–39	6.3	11.7	15.9	11.7	3.4	−1.2
40–44	5.7	11.3	15.6	11.2	3.4	−1.3
45–49	5.3	10.5	15.4	10.5	3.6	−0.3
50–54	5.1	9.5	15.0	10.1	3.6	+1.1
55–59	4.7	8.5	14.2	9.4	3.7	+1.9
60–64	4.4	7.8	13.9	8.8	3.7	+2.7
65 or older	3.5	7.4	13.2	8.5	4.0	+1.9
All	6.2	10.5	15.7	10.9	3.5	+0.9

P_{10} = 10th percentile.　　　$\bar{s}$ = arithmetic mean schooling.
Md = median.　　　　　　　　σ_s = standard deviation.
P_{90} = 90th percentile.　　　$d_u = P_{90} - Md$; $d_1 = Md - P_{10}$.
SOURCE: 1/1,000 sample of U.S. Census, 1960.

distribution of earnings is likely to be positively skewed. As the U.S. level of schooling is the highest in the world, its distribution is more negatively (less positively) skewed than that of any other country. Hence positive skewness in earnings is likely to be universal.

2. The schooling model implies that relative dispersion of earnings is larger the larger the absolute dispersion in the distribution of schooling and the higher the rate of return. In terms of the schooling regression, where the variance in r is suppressed:

$$\sigma^2(\ln Y_s) = r^2\sigma^2(s) + \sigma^2(u). \qquad (3.6)$$

Chiswick's (1967) regional comparisons of income inequality do indeed show that inequality and skewness of income are larger the larger the variance in the distribution of schooling and the higher the rate of return as measured by the size of the regression slope in (1.3). According to Chiswick, these factors jointly explain over a third of the differences in inequality among regions,[18] with the rate of return apparently the more important factor.

Rapid upward trends in years of schooling attainment in the United States are reflected in Table 3.5 in the systematically different distributions of years of schooling in the separate age groups of employed men in 1959. The typical (median) 25-year-old was a high school graduate in 1959, while the typical 60-year-old was an elementary school graduate. Dispersion in the distribution of schooling, as measured by a percentile range or a standard deviation, narrowed somewhat from the older to the younger cohorts, while skewness changed from positive to negative as the level rose.[19]

The systematically larger dispersion and skewness of the schooling distribution with increasing age is paralleled by increases in relative dispersion and skewness in earnings in the age groups, as shown in Tables 3.6 and 6.3. However, the consistency of this phenomenon with predictions of the schooling model is only qualitative: The actual rate of increase of earnings inequality with age is far too strong to be attributable in the main to the mild increase in the dispersion of schooling. The schooling model in variance form (equation 3.6) predicts a smaller percentage increase in $\sigma^2(\ln Y)$ than in $\sigma^2(s)$, if r^2 and $\sigma^2(u)$ do not increase. The variance of schooling is only about 20 per cent larger in the 55–59 age group than in the 30–34 age group (Table 3.5, column 5), yet the variance of relative (log) earnings is 70 per cent greater in the older compared to the younger group[20] (Table 6.3, column 1). The variance of schooling is about 25 per cent larger in the 55–64 age group than in the 25–34 age group in Table 3.5, but the variance of income doubles in this range in every annual

18. In his current work, Chiswick greatly increases the explanatory power of the earnings function by expanding it to include post-school investments. Lydall (1968), who did not employ the rate of return as an explicit variable, found the dispersion in the distribution of schooling to be a significant factor in explaining differences in the inequality of earnings among a set of countries.

19. In their survey of trends in educational attainment of the U.S. *population,* Folger and Nam (1967) found that "educational attainment is more evenly distributed in the population than it used to be." The data in their Chapter 5 show mild trends in dispersion, as well as a pronounced change from positive to negative skewness in the distribution of schooling.

20. As shown in Table 6.3, the relative variance of earnings has a U-shaped age pattern with low values in the 30–34 age group. The age and experience patterns of dispersion are more fully analyzed in Chapter 6.

TABLE 3.6

COHORT AND CROSS-SECTIONAL CHANGES IN INCOME INEQUALITY,

ALL U.S. MEN, 1947–70

(variance of logs of income)

Year	Age			Cross Section (col. 3 less col. 1)	Cohort [a]
	25–34 (1)	35–44 (2)	45–54 (3)		
1947	.352	.494	.541	.189	
1957	.420	.518	.697	.277	
1967	.387	.459	.546	.159	.194
1948	.355	.445	.585	.230	
1958	.445	.489	.727	.282	
1968	.389	.454	.567	.178	.212
1949	.379	.538	.680	.301	
1959	.442	.478	.692	.250	
1969	.418	.469	.572	.154	.193
1950	.378	.471	.642	.254	
1960	.428	.554	.719	.291	
1970	.458	.486	.585	.097	.207
Average				.225	.204

SOURCE: Schultz (1971, Table 2).

a. In each twenty-year span, column 3 of the last year of the span minus column 1 of the first year.

cross section (1947 to 1970) in Table 3.6. The observed age gradient in earnings inequality cannot be ascribed to cohort differences in the distribution of schooling. Rather, it is a phenomenon connected with aging of the same cohort whose distribution of schooling is, of course, fixed.

The within-cohort changes can be observed directly in the repeated cross sections of Table 3.6: Individuals who were 35–44 years old in 1959 were in the 25–34 age group in 1949, and in the 45–54 age group in 1969. Income variances can be compared in the three survey years to detect changes within fixed cohorts. This procedure was applied to variances of logs of income of men in decade age intervals, which were calculated by T. P. Schultz (1971) from Current Population Surveys for the years 1947–70. The results shown in Table 3.6 indicate that the cross-sectional age differences in income inequality were mainly a consequence of changes within the same cohorts.[21] The cross-sectional changes are shown in the rows, the within-cohort changes along the diagonals. As the last two columns show, the cross-sectional increase in inequality is only slightly greater than the within-cohort increase. At the same time there are no clear trends in inequality within fixed age groups.[22] Apparently, the cross-sectional increases in inequality with age are produced, in the main, by factors other than the secular change in the distribution of schooling. The theoretical analysis suggested that an explanation for much of the age difference in parameters of earnings distribution would be found in the distribution of post-school investments. We now proceed to an empirical exploration of the age and experience differences in earnings.

---

21. Very similar results are produced by comparing Gini coefficients, calculated from the same data by H. P. Miller (1963, Table 12). Though the data underlying Table 3.6 are incomes of all men, rather than earnings of nonfarm white men, it is not likely that the conclusions are affected by this inaccuracy. Age patterns of log variances are not very different under the two definitions, though levels of income exceed levels of earnings by 20–30 per cent in each age group.

22. For an analysis of these trends see Chiswick and Mincer (1972).

4

Age and Experience Profiles of Earnings

The experiments reported in the previous section were meant to provide evidence on the extent to which the schooling model is applicable to the analysis of earnings. They indicate the need for caution in extending the schooling model beyond the "overtaking" subset of earnings distributions, even for qualitative analyses. Confidence in the validity of the schooling model as a *component* of human capital analysis is strengthened, but it is necessary to turn to the post-school phase of investment behavior in order to extend the analysis to the whole earnings distribution.

If productivity-augmenting investments in human capital continue after the completion of schooling, the time distribution of these investments over the working life [1] creates age variation in earnings, referred to as the age profile. In proceeding to the empirical analysis of earnings profiles in the light of the investment model, no claim is made, of course, that the observed age profile of an individual re-

---

1. My analysis does not cover the "post-retirement" stage of the life cycle. At that stage, special emphasis must be placed on depreciation of human capital and on the behavior of the labor supply, subjects which are beyond the scope of the present study.

flects only investment behavior. Elements of chance, of changing market opportunities, and of biopsychological development are important. Nonetheless, there is evidence that work experience is much more important than age in affecting productivity and earnings. I interpret productivity-augmenting work experience as an investment phenomenon. The assumption of costless opportunities for augmenting productivity, which is sometimes implied in the notion of "learning by doing," cannot be descriptive of labor markets where labor mobility is the norm rather than the exception.[2] At any rate, the investment interpretation lends itself to empirical analysis. The proper question is how well the investment model handles the data, and whether alternative models can do better.

Given individual differences in investment behavior, earnings profiles differ both among and within schooling groups. I study first the typical shapes of earnings profiles of individuals at a given level of schooling. I then inquire into differences among such *average* earnings profiles of different schooling groups. Later I consider the consequences of *individual* differences in earnings profiles among persons who have the same amount of schooling.

The earnings data shown in Chart 4.1 are mean earnings in the sample of men, by years of schooling and by two-year age intervals up to age 40, and five-year age intervals thereafter.[3] Experience profiles are shown in Chart 4.2. Profiles of annual and weekly earnings in log scales are shown in Charts 4.3 and 4.4. The basic features of the age profiles are easily summarized: except for the initial years of gainful activity, earnings are higher at higher levels of schooling, and increase with age through much of the working life. The absolute and, more consistently, relative rate of increase in annual earnings

---

2. The argument is spelled out by Becker (1964, pp. 45–47): Greater opportunities for learning will attract larger supplies of labor. Consequently, the steeper earnings profiles will shift downward to intersect the flatter ones, giving rise to opportunity costs of learning.

3. Earnings data by single-year intervals were also calculated from the 1/1,000 sample. These showed apparently erratic sawtooth patterns in the profiles, particularly at older ages. This, however, should not be interpreted to mean that typical individual profiles fluctuate erratically over the life cycle. Sample sizes for single years of age and schooling are often quite small. They decrease with age, particularly in higher schooling groups. The pronounced instability of the year-by-year sample averages of earnings can be accounted for by sampling fluctuations as well as earnings variances that are large and increase with age.

CHART 4.1

AGE PROFILES OF EARNINGS OF WHITE, NONFARM MEN, 1959

(annual earnings classified by years of age, for indicated schooling groups)

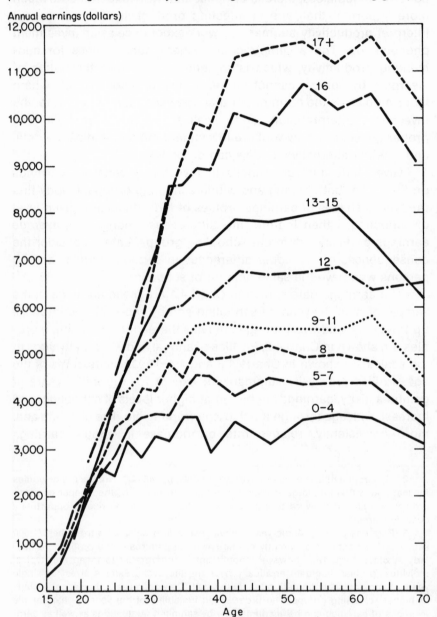

NOTE: Figures on curves indicate years of schooling completed.

SOURCE: 1/1,000 sample of U.S. Census, 1960.

CHART 4.2

EXPERIENCE PROFILES OF EARNINGS OF WHITE, NONFARM MEN, 1959

(annual earnings classified by years of experience, for indicated schooling groups)

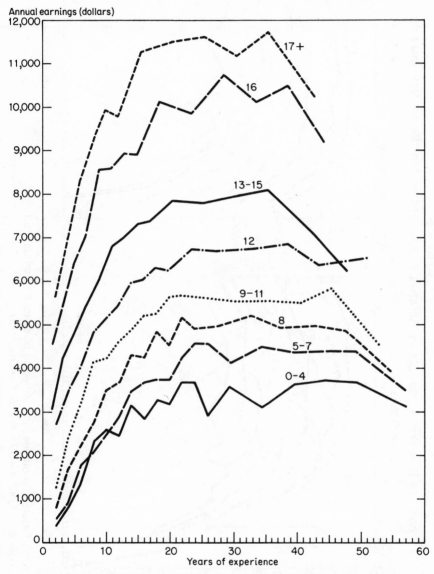

NOTE: Figures on curves indicate years of schooling completed.

SOURCE: 1/1,000 sample of U.S. Census, 1960.

CHART 4.3

AGE AND EXPERIENCE PROFILES OF RELATIVE ANNUAL EARNINGS OF WHITE, NONFARM MEN, 1959

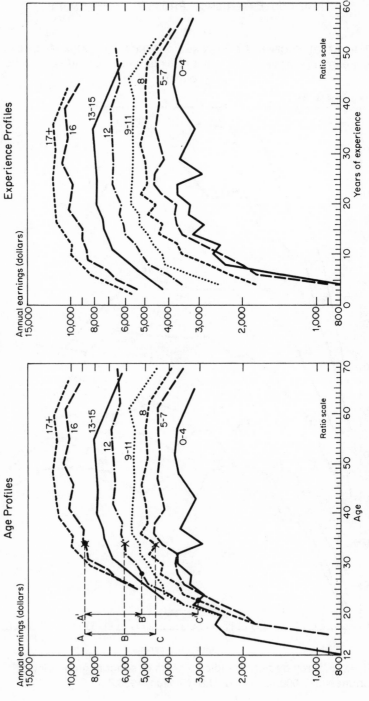

NOTE: Figures on curves indicate years of schooling completed.
SOURCE: 1/1,000 sample of U.S. Census, 1960.

CHART 4.4
AGE AND EXPERIENCE PROFILES OF RELATIVE WEEKLY EARNINGS OF WHITE, NONFARM MEN, 1959

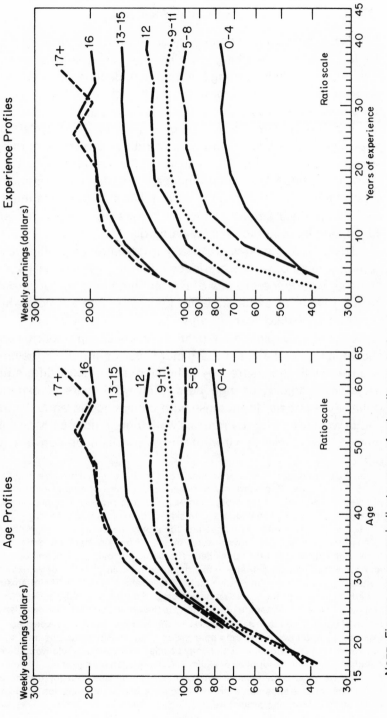

Age Profiles

Experience Profiles

NOTE: Figures on curves indicate years of schooling completed.
SOURCE: 1/1,000 sample of U.S. Census, 1960.

diminishes with age, becoming negative, if it changes at all, during the last decade of working life. There is no visible decline at these later ages in weekly earnings. Apparently, declines in weeks worked per year are the main factor in the decline of annual earnings during the preretirement years (cf. Table 7.2, column 3).

The differences among schooling groups are systematic: *at given ages* the absolute and relative rate of growth of earnings increases with schooling. Earnings level off at earlier ages in the lower schooling groups. Since earnings reach a plateau at later ages in the most highly educated groups, both dollar and relative annual earnings differentials among schooling groups grow with age until age 45–50, and later still for weekly earnings.

The picture changes drastically when earnings profiles are compared by years of work experience rather than age.[4] Chart 4.3 shows that the *experience profiles* of log earnings tend to converge [5] with growing years of experience, in contrast to age profiles, which diverge with growing years of age.

Logarithmic experience profiles of weekly and hourly earnings, shown in Charts 4.4 and 4.5, are more nearly parallel, suggesting that relative "skill" (measured by schooling attainment) differentials in wage rates do not change perceptibly with years of experience.[6] Dollar differentials do increase with experience in annual earnings, and in weekly and hourly rates as well, though not nearly as much as they do with age. In view of the parallelism or convergence of

---

4. Years of experience start at ages indicated in column 3 of Table 3.1.

5. The degree of convergence of experience profiles of *annual* earnings is partly affected by the state of the labor market, since in a recession unemployment rates increase more among the young and unskilled than in other groups.

6. "Skill" differentials in wages are commonly measured by the percentage difference between adult male wage rates in sets of pairs of narrowly defined occupations, one skilled, the other unskilled. The choice of pairs, the definition of wages, and the changing skill contents make the interpretation of such comparisons and of trends in them as trends in relative factor prices rather uncertain. The often steep rise of earnings with age suggests that differing age distributions in the occupations being compared are another source of ambiguity in these measures. For example, an acceleration of upward trends in schooling raises the average age in the lower schooling and skill groups and lowers it in the upper groups. This produces an apparent narrowing of relative wage differentials, which may be misinterpreted as a relative price effect of the change in relative supplies of skills. Standardization for age is not sufficient, however. As we have seen, relative wages increase with age. But my finding of near-parallelism of the experience profiles suggests that standardization for experience is the more appropriate procedure.

CHART 4.5
EXPERIENCE PROFILES OF AVERAGE HOURLY EARNINGS OF WHITE NONFARM
MEN, 1959

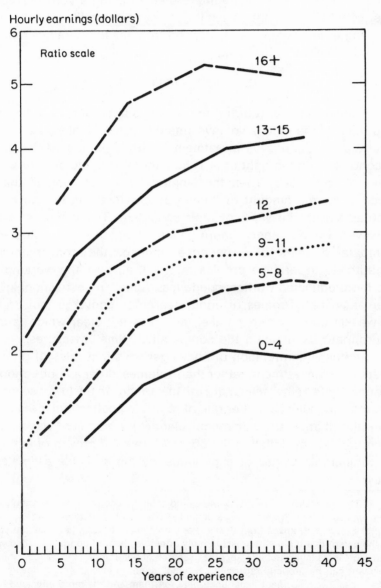

NOTE: Figures on curves indicate years of schooling completed.
SOURCE: Fuchs (1967, Table A-1).

logarithmic experience profiles, the strong increase in relative earnings differentials by age must be attributed entirely to the faster rate of growth of earnings at earlier compared to later years of experience. Let the earnings profiles be interpreted as being a consequence of post-school investments. Then the life-cycle or profile rate of growth g_t of log earnings at time t is derived from the log-earnings function (1.15) in its continuous form:

$$g_t = r_t k_t + \frac{d}{d_t} \ln (1 - k_t). \tag{4.1}$$

Assume rates of return r_t to post-school investment to be fixed, and think of the ratio (k_t) of investment to gross earnings as a "time-equivalent" amount of investment incurred in period t. Let the second term on the right of (4.1) be either negligible or unrelated to levels of schooling. Then the empirical findings suggest that, *at given ages,* the amount of "time" people invest in human capital increases with the years of their schooling. The longer-schooled, however, do not spend more "time" than the less-schooled at *comparable years of experience.* Indeed, the convergence of logarithmic experience profiles means that, over the working life, the more educated workers spend less "time" in post-school investment activities. Profiles of annual earnings converge, but profiles of weekly earnings are parallel, and it is not clear which is more appropriate for gauging the comparative "time" measures.[7]

Another interpretation of convergence is that rates of return to post-school investment, rather than volumes, differ among schooling groups. By (4.1) the steeper growth in earnings in the lower schooling groups may reflect a higher rate of return to post-school investments (r_t) rather than a larger time-equivalent (k_t). An attempt was made to ascertain this by deflating the observed rates of growth of earnings, at comparable stages of experience, by the available estimates of

---

7. The parallelism of weekly earnings indicates that convergence of annual earnings, or the margin by which less schooled persons spend more "time" in post-school investment, arises from their lower employment levels when they are young. To the extent that the greater discontinuity of employment of poorly educated young men represents labor mobility—people in search of better jobs—the periods of unemployment can be properly reckoned as "time" spent in investment. If, however, the differences in employment experience between them and the more educated represent differences in length of involuntary unemployment or in leisure preferences, "time" spent in post-school investments is overstated for the former.

TABLE 4.1
ESTIMATES OF POST-SCHOOL INVESTMENTS IN DOLLARS AND TIME-EQUIVALENTS PER PERSON

Years of Schooling	Dollars $C(10-15)$ (1)	Years $k(10-15)$ (2)	Dollars C_{ps} (3)	Years K_{ps} (4)
0–4	$3,470	1.23	$10,120	3.78
5–7	4,430	1.26	13,350	4.27
8	4,310	1.10	13,570	3.56
9–11	6,000	1.26	14,220	3.10
12	5,920	1.05	15,420	2.68
13–15	7,550	1.09	17,270	2.46
16	8,300	1.09	30,500	3.25

NOTE: Y_p = earnings at peak; Y_s = earnings at overtaking; r = rate of return.

Col. 1: $C(10-15) = (Y_{15} - Y_{10})/r$ = dollar investments between the tenth and fifteenth year of experience.

Col. 2: $k(10-15)$; $(\ln Y_{15} - \ln Y_{10})/r$ = year-equivalents of investment between the tenth and fifteenth year of experience.

Col. 3: $C_{ps} = (Y_p - Y_s)/r$ = total dollar post-school investments.

Col. 4: $K_{ps} = (\ln Y_p - \ln Y_s)/r$ = total year-equivalents of post-school investments.

SOURCE: Earnings data from Charts 4.1–4.3; r from Table 3.1, column 9.

overall rates of return, assuming that they are similar to rates of return on post-school investments. The results, shown in column 2 of Table 4.1, indicate that the deflated slopes decline as schooling level increases, but increase mildly above the high school level.[8]

Table 4.1 also contains estimates of total amounts of net post-school investment incurred by workers in each schooling group over their working life, in dollars and "year-equivalents" (columns 3 and 4). It can be seen that total dollar values rise with schooling, but the time-equivalents are only weakly related to schooling. Total year-equivalents of post-school investment calculated from estimated wage rate data (Chart 4.5) are very similar in all schooling groups and amount to three to four years.

---

8. The observed convergence may also be due to "vintage" or obsolescence effects. Obsolescence diminishes total investment and its rate of decline over time (Becker, Koeune). This is reflected in flatter and less concave earnings profiles, presumably at higher levels of skill (schooling).

TABLE 4.2
ALTERNATIVE ESTIMATES OF POST-SCHOOL INVESTMENT COSTS
PER PERSON, 1939, 1949, 1958

Year	Esti-mates	Years of Schooling								
		8			12			16		
		C_s	C_{ps}	K_{ps}	C_s	C_{ps}	K_{ps}	C_s	C_{ps}	K_{ps}
1958	Old	2.2	4.9		2.8	7.6		24.1	28.8	
	New		9.2	3.9		11.7	2.9		22.9	3.3
1949	Old	1.8	4.4		6.4	9.7		18.0	27.4	
	New		8.2	3.8		15.4	4.2		30.9	4.4
1939	Old	1.3	3.9		5.2	8.5		14.7	15.2	
	New		7.0	4.6		14.1	4.9		17.8	3.6

C_s = investment in schooling in constant dollars (thousands).
C_{ps} = post-school investment in constant dollars (thousands).
K_{ps} = post-school investment in year-equivalents.
SOURCE: Mincer (1962, Table 1 and appendix data).

In a previous study, dollar estimates of post-school investment were calculated in a stepwise fashion by estimating instalments of such investments (Mincer, 1962). The totals in dollars and time-equivalents are here re-estimated from the same data, and a comparison of the old and new estimates is shown in Table 4.2.

The old estimates are very similar to the new at the college level, but about half the size at lower levels, primarily because the 0–4 schooling group age profile was used as the "zero investment" base line in the disaggregated procedure. It is difficult to believe that individuals in the lowest schooling group incur no post-school investments, but it may also be argued that the "no-investment" profile is not horizontal but concave, for biological reasons. It is perhaps best, therefore, to consider the alternative estimates in Table 4.2 as bracketing the true values. This would mean, in turn, that the time-equivalents in the table are also overstated somewhat, particularly at the lower levels of schooling. If the time values are midway between the two estimates, the dollar volumes of post-school investment are overstated 20–25 per cent on average when a horizontal shape is assumed for the zero investment profile.

The investment behavior inferred from the earnings profiles, though in some respects unclear, is quite plausible in the light of human capital theory. The logarithmic concavity of the earnings profiles is actually strongly implied by the analysis of optimal distribution of human capital investments over the life cycle.[9]

The differences among schooling groups are plausible: those who invest more (dollars) in schooling also spend more in post-school investments. Greater ability and better access to financing opportunities are common factors in both forms of investment. These factors evidently dominate whatever incentives and opportunities exist for substitution between the two kinds of investment. As for time-equivalent measures of investment, the cross-sectional figures in Tables 4.1 and 4.2 indicate a negative or zero correlation between time spent in schooling and in post-school investments. Over time, total schooling and post-school investments grew in dollar terms. However, schooling expenditures grew more rapidly than expenditures on post-school investments (compare C_s with C_{ps} in Table 4.2). The growth of public subsidies to education may have been an important incentive for substituting schooling for job training. In time units, this substitution accelerated the upward trend in years of schooling and reduced somewhat the time spent in job training.

The empirical findings about levels and shapes of the average earnings profiles in the different schooling groups imply the following intergroup differentials in earnings:

1. Dollar differentials among schooling groups increase with experience. Because the earnings profiles are concave, the increase is much more pronounced with age.

2. Relative intergroup differentials in annual earnings grow with age, but diminish with experience. Weekly and hourly relative wage differentials among schooling groups do not perceptibly change with experience. Given a sufficiently small decline in differentials by experience, the increase by age is due to a strong logarithmic concavity of the earnings profiles. As already explained, concavity of earnings reflects diminishing investments over the working life.

The intergroup differentials account for only a part of the total inequality (variance) among individuals within age or experience groups intragroup dispersion — differentials in earnings among indi-

---

9. See Becker (1967, Part I, Chap. 1), and Ben-Porath (1968).

viduals of the same schooling and age—is the other component of the variance. Because both components of inequality are large, we cannot explain variances in age or schooling subgroups without a prior analysis of ungrouped, individual data.[10]

Before we proceed to an econometric analysis of earnings profiles, it will be useful to consider somewhat more closely two important qualifications to the investment interpretation of earnings profiles: (1) The allocation of investment over the life cycle cannot be simply "read into" the *cross-sectional* profiles, which represent earnings differences among distinct individuals who differ by age. Though they had the same years of schooling, the different cohorts may have had different patterns of post-school experience.[11] (2) The life-cycle earnings profile partly reflects biopsychological development: of maturation at young ages and decline at older ages. This development is systematic and largely independent of (exogenous to) the individual's will. To the extent that this development creates a concave earnings profile, the investment interpretation must be modified.

Granted the validity of these qualifications in principle, their weight remains to be settled on empirical grounds: (1) How different are cohort earnings profiles from cross-sectional profiles in the same schooling groups, abstracting from economywide fluctuations and secular trends? (2) How important are the "inherent" age effects in the observed earnings profiles? Empirical evidence is needed to indicate whether we are dealing with major objections or minor qualifications. Scanty though it is, some evidence on the matter is available, and it bears consideration:

1. In a study based on annual income data of the Current Population Survey, H. P. Miller calculated average annual age-income profiles of U.S. men in each of the several schooling groups for

---

10. In my analysis of 1950 data (Mincer, 1957, 1958), variances in age and schooling groups were explained only in terms of intergroup differentials observed in typical earnings profiles. No contradiction arises in dollar variances, but the structure of relative variances is more intricate, as will be shown.

11. It should be clear, however, that even if major problems were to be posed by the differences between cohorts and cross sections and between "autonomous" and investment-induced components of earnings profiles, they do not represent arguments against a human capital analysis. When better understood, these phenomena can and will be incorporated into the human capital models.

1956–66. Cohort changes in income can be calculated from these data by comparing pairs of cross sections. Individuals in a given schooling group who were 25 years old in 1956 were 35 in 1966. In Chart 4.6, the percentage rate of growth of their income in this period is the ordinate of the upper (solid) line corresponding to age 25 on the horizontal scale, while the ordinate of the lower (broken) line at this point shows the growth rate from age 25 to 35 in the 1956 cross section.[12]

The upper and lower lines are similar in shape, i.e., cohort profiles are similar in shape to the cross sections. They are displaced upward by some 20–30 per cent per decade in most schooling groups and ages, that is, actual growth of income was that much greater in each cohort than in the cross section—a common effect of economy-wide secular growth.

Table 4.3 shows the vertical displacement of the cohort from the cross-sectional profiles at selected ages in the several schooling groups. The variation in these numbers may reflect "non-neutrality" in income growth, in favor of more educated and younger males, or it may represent a relative understatement in the cross section of the cohort post-school investments of these groups. Whichever the correct interpretation may be, the concavity of logarithmic profiles is evident in cohorts. Indeed, the suggested non-neutrality would result in more pronounced concavity in the cohort than in the cross section and a greater divergence of profiles with advancing age.

2. Studies of 1964 and 1966 earnings of economists and a companion study of 1966 earnings of all full-time employed persons reported to the National Register of Scientific and Technical Personnel[13] included data on years of professional work experience in addition to six other characteristics: age, years of schooling, profession, type of employer, work activity, and sex.

Economists of the same years of schooling and age had a considerable dispersion of years of work experience: About 20 per cent

---

12. The years 1956 and 1966 were chosen because of their similar cyclical positions. The use of income rather than earnings is a minor drawback.

13. The 1964 study is reported in Tolles et al. (1965). The studies are based on over 10,000 reports from economists, and over 200,000 reports from all personnel in the Register. The very informative multivariate statistical analysis of the data was designed and carried out by E. Melichar of the Federal Reserve Board.

CHART 4.6
AGE PROFILES OF DECADAL PERCENTAGE CHANGES IN MALE INCOMES, BY
SCHOOLING COHORTS, 1956–66, AND IN CROSS SECTION, 1956

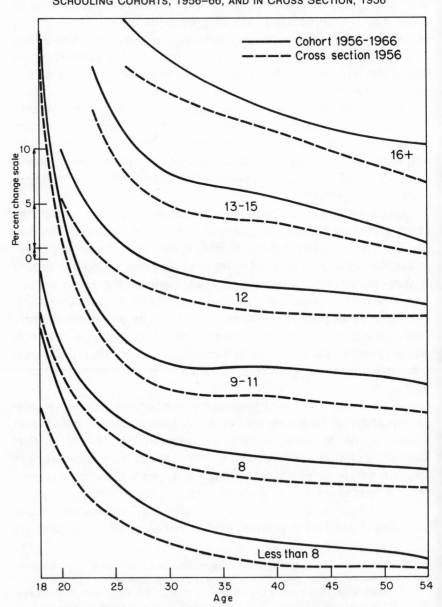

NOTE: Figures on curves indicate years of schooling completed.
SOURCE: U.S. Bureau of the Census (August 1968, Table 11).

TABLE 4.3
ANNUAL GROWTH RATE OF INCOME OF MEN IN SELECTED AGE
AND SCHOOLING GROUPS, 1956–66
(income in 1966 dollars)

Age in 1956	Under 8	8	9–11	12	13–15	16 or More
			Years of Schooling			
25	3.2%	2.2%	2.4%	2.7%	3.5%	4.0%
30	2.3	2.1	2.4	2.4	3.0	3.1
35	2.2	2.1	2.6	2.3	3.1	2.2
40	2.2	2.1	2.7	2.3	2.4	1.7
45	1.8	1.8	2.8	2.0	1.9·	2.1
50	1.4	1.8	2.8	1.6	1.7	2.5

SOURCE: U.S. Census (1968, Table 11).

of persons in the same five-year age interval differed by more than 10 years of work experience (Tolles et al., 1965, Table 7, p. 40). This variability and the large sample sizes permitted a statistically significant separation of the effects of age and of experience on earnings. Correlation of log earnings of economists with years of experience yielded an R^2 of .41; correlation with years of age yielded $R^2 = .23$. For all scientists, the simple coefficient of determination of earnings with experience was .34; with age, it was .24. In the multiple regressions on the seven characteristics, length of professional experience and schooling (measured by highest degree) were the two most powerful, and age was the least important, variable (Tolles and Melichar, 1968, Table II-2, p. 60; and Tolles et al., 1965, p. 64).

The studies showed that for economists under the age of 35, five additional years of age provided a $300–$400 advantage, given the same length of experience, while an additional five years of experience were associated with a gain of $1,500–$2,000, given the same age (Tolles et al., 1965, p. 42). If so, the net age effect is about 20 per cent of the combined effect of age and experience on earnings at the younger ages. The net incremental value (partial regression coefficient) of years of experience declined as length of service increased, but the increments remained positive throughout the observed working lives (Tolles et al., 1965, pp. 43, 49, 50).

The partial regression coefficient of age showed a decelerating progression of salary with age which continued to about age 50, and then became negative, that is, a net decline was associated with advancing age (Tolles et al., 1965, p. 70). Compared to the gross effect, the net effect of age was quite small, but the net effect of experience was almost as large as the gross effect (Tolles et al., 1965, Figure 1, pp. 66–67).

The findings for all scientific professions are similar to those for economists. The observed experience profiles of earnings differ a great deal among specialities, type of employer, and type of work activity. These differences can be attributed to the differential effects of experience.

If we interpret the contribution of years of experience as investment-induced effects on earnings, and the contribution of age as the "inherent" effects of biopsychological individual development, the quantitative evidence of the AEA studies strongly supports the interpretation of observed earnings profiles in terms of investment in human capital.

It is important to note, however, that the "age effect," small though it is, contributes to the concavity of the observed earnings profiles. If ignored, as it is perforce in the current study, investment is overstated somewhat (20 per cent was suggested above) at ages below 35, though understated later.[14]

Even if experience is shown to be a much more powerful determinant of earnings than age, nevertheless an objection to the investment interpretation of the earnings profile could be made on the ground that the growth of earnings with experience may reflect the prevalence of institutional arrangements such as seniority provisions in employment practices. Such practices, however, do not contradict the productivity-augmenting investment hypothesis, unless it can be shown that growth of earnings under seniority provisions is largely independent of productivity growth.[15]

A recent BLS study, *Seniority in Promotion and Transfer Provisions,* makes clear that this is not the case. The study is based on an examination of virtually all major collective bargaining agreements (1,851 in all), each covering 1,000 workers or more (exclusive

---

14. This is comparable to the conclusions reached on the basis of Table 4.2.
15. In this study, productivity growth is not assumed to be costless.

of railroads, airlines, and government). The majority of the agreements, covering over 70 per cent of workers subject to the agreements, contain specific provisions for promotions. The absence of such provisions is typical of industries with one or more of the following characteristics: (1) Sharply differentiated skills and upward movement to journeyman status through apprenticeship; (2) labor agreements where no promotion is possible within the bargaining unit; and (3) relatively high enterprise mortality, employee turnover, or sporadic or seasonal employment (*Seniority*, p. 3). Promotion based *only* on seniority occurred in agreements covering less than 2 per cent of workers (*Seniority*, p. 5). In all other cases seniority was considered *jointly* with merit, skill, aptitude, and other factors. Seniority was cited as a *principal* factor in agreements covering 20 per cent of the workers. However, in agreements covering 50 per cent of the workers, seniority applied only if other qualifying factors were the same among the employees being considered for promotion. A typical clause is:

When a vacancy occurs in one of the higher rate crafts, employees with seniority shall be given full consideration before an appointment is made; however, seniority shall not be the governing factor and shall not prevent the transfer or appointment of an employee with less seniority, whose ability and qualifications are greater than those of the senior employee under consideration for the work on the higher paid job (*Seniority*, p. 6).

Seniority is more important as a factor in promotion of blue-collar than of white-collar workers. It is least important in the professional, technical, sales, and supervisory categories of jobs. Skill and ability are the principal nonseniority factors in agreements covering about 75 per cent of the workers. Education is mentioned in only about 7 per cent of the agreements as a factor in promotion.

In most of the agreements the employer is required to make selections for promotion from the group of employees who had expressed an interest in the vacancy. In some agreements promotion is restricted to specific employees in a line of progression, but such "automatic" promotions are largely confined to smaller or narrower job units—usually with a narrow occupational classification. A few agreements call for tests to be administered to workers applying for promotion. Many call for a (1–2 months) trial and training period on the new job. Such a period allows the company to determine whether the employee can perform the job satisfactorily and gives the employee time to decide whether the job suits him. The bid for promotion can be costly: disqualification during the probationary period is considered in most of the agreements, and while in most of them the disqualified worker is allowed to return to his previous job, in some penalties are attached, such as some loss of seniority rights, and even downward job transfers (*Seniority,* p. 31).

Long training periods following the promotion were in most instances unnecessary, since employees covered by the provisions (unlike those in formal training or apprenticeship programs) ordinarily had acquired the necessary skills in lower-rated jobs, or were advanced through a series of semiskilled tasks requiring relatively little training at each step. This situation is a vivid demonstration of the processes of accumulation of human capital on the job.

In sum, it appears that productivity is a major criterion for promotion in rules developed in collective bargaining. Moreover, the confinement of "automatic" promotion to narrow job classifications is an indication that productivity growth looms larger the bigger the job advancement.

The negligible role of school education in promotion is consistent with the view that post-school productivity growth is causally related not to schooling but to post-school investments. This view was supported by evidence (Table 3.4, above) of a declining correlation between schooling and earnings as work experience accumulates.

5

The Human Capital
Earnings Function

5.1   EMPIRICAL SPECIFICATION

The interpretation of age and experience profiles of earnings as consequences of investment behavior makes it possible to expand the schooling model to include post-school investments in an econometric analysis of the distribution of earnings.

The importance of the life-cycle distribution of post-school investments in creating earnings inequality is empirically quite obvious: As Charts 4.1–4.3 show, annual earnings nearly double after two to three decades of experience in each schooling group, a differential almost as great as that between the earnings of males with 8 and 16 years of schooling. It is, of course, known from previous work, not tied to human capital analysis, that the inclusion of age in addition to schooling in a multivariate regression analysis of earnings increases the explanatory power of the analysis. It is also known that since age interacts with schooling in affecting earnings (in dollars and in logs), a linear additive form of regression without interaction terms is not adequate. Now, we have not only obtained a behavioral interpretation of this interaction but also noticed that there is less of an interaction, if any, between experience and schooling than between age and schooling: experience profiles of log earnings are much more nearly parallel than age profiles. If so, in an earnings function in which earnings are logarithmic, years of work experience should be entered additively[1] and in arithmetical form. The experience term is, of course, not linear, but concave. For example (see formulation 5.2a, below) the earnings function might be parabolic in the experience term:

$$\ln E_t = \ln E_s + \beta_1 t - \beta_2 t^2,$$

where t is years of experience and E_s is earning capacity after completion of schooling. Since

$$\ln E_s = \ln E_0 + rs;$$

$$\ln E_t = \ln E_0 + rs + \beta_1 t - \beta_2 t^2.$$

If work experience is continuous and starts immediately after completion of schooling, then work experience is equal to current age minus age at completion of schooling; $t = (A - s - b)$, where A is current age and b is age at the beginning of schooling. Thus, the use of age alone instead of experience in the earnings function results in the omission of some variables, as can be seen if the expression for t, above, is substituted in the function:

$$\ln E_t = \ln E_0 + rs + \beta_1(A - s - b) + \beta_2(A - s - b)^2.$$

The quadratic term leaves out an age-schooling interaction variable (As). What is more, the partial omission of s leads to a change in its coefficient which can no longer be interpreted as a rate of return to schooling.[2]

---

1. The possibility of interaction between experience and schooling is explored in the regression analysis in the next section.

2. The coefficient is biased downward. A simplified example is (cf. Griliches and Mason, 1972):

$$\ln Y = \alpha_0 + \alpha_1 s + \alpha_2 A.$$

Neglecting the quadratic term also in the alternative specification

$$\ln Y = \alpha + rs + \beta t,$$

and substituting $t = (A - s - b)$, yields

$$\ln Y = (\alpha - \beta b) + (r - \beta)s + \beta A.$$

Thus α_1 is an underestimate of r.

The proper form of the experience function depends on the form of the life-cycle investment function. The economic theory of optimizing behavior implies that investment in human capital declines over the life cycle, at least beyond an early stage. Apart from this, economic theory provides no guidance to the specific form of the investment function. Accordingly, a few simple specifications of investment profiles are introduced here. From these, earnings functions are derived which are applied, in the next section, to the individual data in an analysis of the entire cross section of male earnings in 1959.

Mathematical simplicity and statistical tractability call for a consideration of linear and log-linear experience functions (profiles) of net dollar investments (C_t) and "time-equivalent" investment ratios (k_t). Four simple specifications are considered:

$$(5.1) \qquad C_t = C_0 - \frac{C_0}{T} t \qquad\qquad (5.3) \qquad C_t = C_0 e^{-\beta t}$$

$$(5.2) \qquad k_t = k_0 - \frac{k_0}{T} t \qquad\qquad (5.4) \qquad k_t = k_0 e^{-\beta t}$$

C_0 and k_0 are the instalments of investment and investment ratios during the initial period of experience, $t = 0$. T is the total period of positive net investment; [3] e, the base of natural logs; and β, a parameter indicating the rate of decline of investment.

It is convenient, at this point, to treat the investment and earnings functions as continuous functions of time. The "gross" dollar earnings function is:

$$E_t = E_s + r_t \int_{j=0}^{t} C_j dj, \tag{a}$$

where E_s denotes earnings obtainable after s years of schooling with no further investments, and r_t is the rate of return to post-school investment, which is assumed to be equal in all periods t.

The logarithmic version is:

$$\ln E_t = \ln E_s + r_t \int_{j=0}^{t} k_j dj. \tag{b}$$

---

3. T need not be specified a priori. It is implicit in the statistically estimated parameters.

By substitution of specifications (5.1) and (5.3) into the arithmetical earnings function (a), and (5.2) and (5.4) into the logarithmic function (b), the earnings functions are transformed from functions containing investment variables (C_t or k_t) that cannot be observed into functions of years of experience,[4] which can be observed and can therefore be used in empirical analysis. Since observed earnings are more akin to "net" earnings (Y_t) than to "gross" earnings, E_t must first be transformed into Y_t by letting $Y_t = E_t - C_t$, and $\ln Y_t = \ln E_t + \ln (1 - k_t)$.

I now derive the empirically observable earnings functions corresponding to the four specifications of investment profiles:

1. The assumption of a linear decline in dollar net investments yields the gross earnings function:

$$E_t = E_s + rC_0 t - \frac{rC_0}{2T} t^2; \tag{5.1a}$$

and the net earnings function:

$$Y_t = (E_s - C_0) + C_0 \left(r + \frac{1}{T}\right) t - \frac{rC_0}{2T} t^2. \tag{5.1b}$$

Here both the dollar earnings profiles are parabolic in years of experience (t). Note also that the time derivative of E_t and Y_t, that is, the dollar increment of earnings, is a linearly declining function of time.

2. If the investment ratio is assumed to decline linearly, the gross log-earnings function becomes parabolic:

$$\ln E_t = \ln E_s + rk_0 t - \frac{rk_0}{2T} t^2; \tag{5.2a}$$

and the net earnings function becomes:

$$\ln Y_t = \ln E_s + rk_0 t - \frac{rk_0}{2T} t^2 + \ln (1 - k_t). \tag{5.2b}$$

In this case, the logarithmic increment in earnings is only approximately a linear declining function of time.

---

4. Years of experience were directly observed in the AEA study of economists' earnings. Direct information is, unfortunately, not available in the Census data. In the current study, therefore, the "observable" is only an imperfect estimate. Its construction was shown in columns 1 and 3 of Table 3.1.

3. If dollar investments decline exponentially with increased experience, then the earnings functions are:

$$E_t = E_s + \frac{rC_0}{\beta} - \frac{rC_0}{\beta} e^{-\beta t} \tag{5.3a}$$

and

$$Y_t = E_s + \frac{rC_0}{\beta} - \frac{(r+\beta)C_0}{\beta} e^{-\beta t}. \tag{5.3b}$$

Here, both dollar earnings and dollar increments of earnings are exponential in t. The logarithm of the increment is linear, since

$$\frac{dY_t}{dt} = (r+\beta)C_0 e^{-\beta t}. \tag{5.3c}$$

In discrete form:

$$Y_{t+1} - Y_t = \frac{(r+\beta)C_0}{\beta} e^{-\beta t}(1 - e^{-\beta}).$$

Let $e^{-\beta} = \gamma$ and $E_s + (rC_0/\beta) = E_p$ (peak earnings). Then

$$Y_{t+1} - Y_t = (1 - \gamma)(E_p - Y_t)$$

and

$$Y_{t+1} = (1 - \gamma)E_p + \gamma Y_t. \tag{5.3d}$$

According to (5.3d), dollar earnings follow a first-order linear autoregression.

4. Finally, if the investment ratio declines exponentially, then the earnings functions are:

$$\ln E_t = \ln E_s + \frac{rk_0}{\beta} - \frac{rk_0}{\beta} e^{-\beta t} \tag{5.4a}$$

and

$$\ln Y_t = \ln E_s + \frac{rk_0}{\beta} - \frac{rk_0}{\beta} e^{-\beta t} + \ln (1 - k_0 e^{-\beta t}). \tag{5.4b}$$

The gross earnings function (5.4a) is the familiar modified Gompertz curve. The percentage increments $d(\ln E_t)/dt$ are exponential, while $d(\ln Y_t)/dt$ are approximately so.

Here also:

$$\ln E_{t+1} - \ln E_t = (1 - \gamma)(\ln E_p - \ln E_t) \tag{5.4c}$$

and

$$\ln E_{t+1} = (1 - \gamma) \ln E_p + \gamma \ln E_t. \tag{5.4d}$$

The Gompertz earnings function (5.4c) is equivalent to a Koyck adjustment equation in logs (5.4c) and follows a log-linear first-order autoregression (5.4d). The net earnings function (5.4b) is approximately Gompertz, and has the corresponding approximate properties.

For regression analysis, the logarithmic forms (5.2b) and (5.4b) are preferable, because the schooling investment data used in this study are in years. This requires the use of $\ln E_s(= \ln E_0 + r_s s)$ rather than E_s in the earnings function. Also, as was noted above, the logarithmic form minimizes the need for interaction terms, permitting an application of the same estimating equation to the whole cross section.

The parameter estimates in the earnings function can also be interpreted in terms of gross rather than net investment, if a fixed depreciation rate δ is assumed. As was shown in Part I, equation (1.21), the general earnings function in those terms is:

$$\ln E_t = \ln E_0 + (r - \delta)s + r \int_{j=0}^{t} (k_j^* - \delta j)dj,$$

where k^* is the gross investment ratio. For example, the parabolic earnings function becomes:

$$\ln E_t = \ln E_0 + (r - \delta)s + (rk_0^* - \delta)t - \frac{rk_0^*}{2T^*} t^2, \tag{5.2e}$$

where T^* is the gross investment period; and the corresponding Gompertz function is:

$$\ln E_t = \ln E_0 + (r - \delta)s - \delta t + r \frac{k_0^*}{\beta} (1 - e^{-\beta t}). \tag{5.4e}$$

Some empirical analyses of earnings relate dollar earnings to years of schooling. This is a misspecification from the point of view of the human capital model. In the NSF study, described in the preceding chapter, it was reported that logarithms of earnings yielded stronger statistical fits than dollar earnings when related to years of schooling and experience.[5]

Another form of earnings function, which is not derived from a human capital model, was used in a recent study by Thurow (1970). He used the log of schooling, instead of years of schooling, in the regression with earnings in logs:

$$\ln Y_t = a + b \ln s + c \ln t.$$

Goodness of fit cannot be compared because the function was fitted by Thurow to averages of groups, not to microdata. However, Heckman and Polachek fitted it at the microlevel and found the fit inferior to specification (5.2b), above. Apparently, also, the rate of return to schooling is underestimated in the Thurow equation, and the returns to experience are substantially overstated.[6]

5.2   REGRESSION ANALYSIS OF INDIVIDUAL EARNINGS

We are now ready to apply the human capital earnings function to the cross-sectional distribution of individual earnings. The specification of that function relates the distribution of logs of earnings to the distribution of cumulated ratios of investment to gross earnings. If the post-school investment profile can be summarized by a pair of parameters, k_0 and β, as in equation (5.4), then the earnings function will involve the variables s and t and the parameters r_s, r_t, k_0, and β, where r_s and r_t are rates of return to schooling and to post-school investments, k_0 is the initial post-school investment ratio, and β is its rate of decline:

$$\ln Y_{i,t} = \ln E_{0i} + r_{si}s_i + f(t/k_{0i}, \beta_i, r_{ti}) + \epsilon_i. \tag{5.5}$$

---

5. Multiple R^2 was .55 for log earnings compared to .41 for dollar values (Tolles et al., p. 65). The goodness of fit could not be directly compared. However, statistical tests devised by Box and Cox (1964) confirm the superiority of the logarithmic dependent variable in the earnings regressions based on the Census 1/1,000 sample, reported in the next section. See Heckman and Polachek (1972).

6. Since $r_s = \partial \ln Y/\partial s$, and $b = \partial \ln Y/\partial \ln s$, $r_s = b/\bar{s} = .72/11 = .06$ in the 9-to-12-year schooling group. This is half the size of my estimates. At the same time $r_p k = \partial \ln Y/\partial t = Ct = .65$ over the 6-to-15-year experience range. Since k cumulated over this range is not likely to exceed 2 — it is less than 2 in the first decade of experience according to Table 4.1, above — the implicit estimate of r_p, the rate of return to post-school experience, is very high.

If information were available on all variables and parameters for each individual i, the equation would represent a complete accounting (short of the random factor ϵ_i) of the human capital characteristics entering into the formation of earnings.

Of course, the availability of such information is not even conceivable. A more modest research objective is to abstract from individual variation in initial earning capacity (ln E_{0i}) and in rates of return on investments, and consider only the effects of the *volume* of investment on earnings. Average parameters ln E_0, r_s, and r_t would then appear in the statistically estimated coefficients of equation (5.6):

$$\ln Y_{i,t} = \ln E_0 + r_s s_i + f(t/k_{0i}, \beta_i, r_t) + u_i. \tag{5.6}$$

Individual variation in r_{si}, r_{ti}, and ln E_{0i} would be impounded in u_i.

Unfortunately, while information on schooling attainment s_i is available for each individual, this is not true for post-school investment. Differences in quantities of post-school investment among individuals are given by differences in k_{0i} and β_i in addition to differences in years of experience. It is therefore necessary to suppress the index i inside the experience function f, and use as the earnings function:

$$\ln Y_{i,t} = \ln E_0 + r_s s_i + f(t/k_0, \beta, r_t) + v_i. \tag{5.7}$$

The data selected from the 1/1,000 sample which were usable for the regression analysis were 31,093 observations of annual earnings in 1959 of white, nonfarm, nonstudent men up to age 65. Parabolic and Gompertz functions [equations (5.2b) and (5.4b) of the preceding section] were fitted to this set, as well as to a somewhat smaller set (28,678 observations) consisting of earnings in each of 40 years after completion of schooling. Here, the oldest age was 55 for men with 8 years of schooling and 64 for those with 16 years of schooling. The variance of log earnings in the (40 years of) experience set was 0.668, compared to 0.694 in the age (under 65) set.

The parabolic and Gompertz estimating equations were specified to a quadratic approximation in a Taylor expansion. Formulated in terms of net investments the parabolic earnings function,

$$\ln Y_t = \ln E_0 + r_s s_i + r_t k_0 t - \frac{r_t k_0}{2T} t^2 + \ln \left(1 - k_0 + \frac{k_0}{T} t\right), \tag{5.2b}$$

is estimated by

$$\ln Y_t = a + b_1 s + b_2 t + b_3 t^2 + v, \tag{P}$$

where

$$a = \ln E_0 - k_0 \left(1 + \frac{k_0}{2}\right); \qquad b_2 = r_t k_0 + \frac{k_0}{T}(1 + k_0);$$

$$b_1 = r_s; \qquad\qquad b_3 = -\left[\frac{r_t k_0}{2T} + \frac{(k_0)^2}{2T^2}\right].$$

The Gompertz earnings function,

$$\ln Y_t = \ln E_0 + \frac{r_t k_0}{\beta} + r_s s - \frac{r k_0}{\beta} e^{-\beta t} + \ln (1 - k_0 e^{-\beta t}), \tag{5.4b}$$

is estimated by:

$$\ln Y_t = a + b_1 s + b_2 x_t + b_3 x_t^2 + v, \tag{G}$$

where

$$x_t = e^{-\beta t}; \qquad b_2 = -\frac{r_t k_0}{\beta} - k_0;$$

$$a = \ln E_0 + \frac{r_t k_0}{\beta}; \qquad b_3 = -\frac{k_0^2}{2}.$$

$$b_1 = r_s;$$

When earnings are expressed as a function of gross investment, k_0^* replaces k_0, T^* replaces T, and $-\delta$ is an additional term in the coefficients b_1 and b_2.

Table 5.1 contains the estimated parabolic (P) and Gompertz (G) regression equations and multiple coefficients of determination of the earnings distribution for forty years of experience.[7]

All the estimated coefficients shown in Table 5.1 are highly significant in a sampling sense: the coefficients are many times larger than their standard errors. This is due to the very large sample size, though size alone is not a sufficient condition for statistical significance.

The coefficient of determination R^2 is of special interest as an

---

7. The regression results of the under-65 age distribution are not presented. The regression coefficients in the age cross section were very close to those in the experience cross section, but the multiple coefficients of determination were .02–.03 points lower in the age set in both the parabolic and Gompertz formulations.

TABLE 5.1
REGRESSIONS OF INDIVIDUAL EARNINGS ON SCHOOLING (s),
EXPERIENCE (x), AND WEEKS WORKED (W)
(1959 annual earnings of white, nonfarm men)

Equation Forms	R^2
S(1) $\ln Y = 7.58 + .070s$ (43.8)	.067
P(1) $\ln Y = 6.20 + .107s + .081t - .0012t^2$ (72.3) (75.5) (−55.8)	.285
P(2) $\ln Y = 4.87 + .255s - .0029s^2 - .0043ts + .148t - .0018t^2$ (23.4) (−7.1) (−31.8) (63.7) (−66.2)	.309
P(3) $\ln Y = f(D_s) + .068t - .0009t^2 + 1.207 \ln W$ (13.1) (10.5) (119.7)	.525
G(1a) $\ln Y = 7.43 + .110s - 1.651x_{at}$ (77.6) (−102.3)	.313
G(1b) $\ln Y = 7.52 + .113s - 1.521x_{bt}$ (74.3) (−101.4)	.307
G(2a) $\ln Y = 7.43 + .108s - 1.172x_{at} - .324x_{at}^2 + 1.183 \ln W$ (65.4) (−16.8) (−10.2) (105.4)	.546
G(2b) $\ln Y = 7.50 + .111s - 1.291x_{bt} - .162x_{bt}^2 + 1.174 \ln W$ (65.0) (−3.5) (−16.0) (107.3)	.551
G(3) $\ln Y = f(D_{s,x}) + 1.142 \ln W$ (108.1)	.557
G(4) $\ln Y = 7.53 + .109s - 1.192x_{bt} - .146x_{bt}^2 - .012t + 1.155 \ln W$ (−2.4)	.556

NOTE: Figures in parentheses are t ratios. R^2 = coefficient of determination; S = linear form; P = parabolic form; G = Gompertz form; $D_{s,x}$ = dummies for schooling and experience; $x_{at} = e^{-.15t}$, $x_{bt} = e^{-.10t}$; W = weeks worked during 1959.

estimate of the fraction of earnings inequality that is associated with the distribution of human capital investments. The regression coefficients are not the primary concern in this study. They do, however, represent an important check on the consistency of the interpretation of the regression equations as human capital earnings functions.

5.3   MAJOR FINDINGS OF THE REGRESSION ANALYSIS

1. Equations (P1), (G1), and (G2) specify the same shape of logarithmic experience functions for each individual, permitting only dif-

ferences in levels. They also specify the same rate of return to schooling for all. Despite these strong restrictions, the two variables s and t alone explain about 30 per cent — 28.5 per cent in (P), 32 per cent in (G) — of aggregate earnings inequality.

2. Relaxation of these restrictions is achieved in a parametric fashion in (P2): Here the s^2 term is added to allow for systematically different rates of return to schooling at different levels of schooling. The results are statistically significant and already familiar: the coefficient at s^2 is negative, indicating a lower rate of return to schooling at higher levels of schooling.

A similar nonparametric relaxation is obtained in (G3) by use of dummy variables. These yield separate intercepts for each schooling level. They are not shown in the table, as their features are the same as those already seen in (P2).

3. The partial coefficient of schooling is an estimate of the average rate of return to schooling. The marginal rates are approximated in nonlinear formulations, such as (P2), which permit the estimation of different rates at different levels of schooling. In (P2), the marginal rates:

$$r_s = \frac{d \ln Y}{ds} = .255 - .0058s - .0043t,$$

when estimated at $t = 8$ (roughly at overtaking), are 17.4 per cent at 8 years of schooling, 15.1 per cent at 12 years, and 12.8 per cent at 16 years.

The negative coefficient of the interaction term (st) describes the apparent convergence of experience profiles. Both the nonlinearity of s and the interaction st become insignificant when weeks worked is included in the regressions, such as (P2) and (G2). The same behavior of s^2 was observed in the overtaking set (cf. Table 3.3); and the parallelism of weekly earnings (no interaction st), in Chart 4.4.

4. The experience variable $x_t = e^{-\beta t}$ in the Gompertz equations was iterated for β, the rate of decline of time-equivalent investments, between 0.30 and 0.05 in 0.05 intervals. The highest R^2 and most plausible coefficient values were found in the 0.10–0.15 range. While R^2 changes little in a wider interval, the partial regression coefficients are sensitive to the specification of β. The coefficient at the quadratic term is particularly unstable when different values of β are tried.

At any rate, k_0 and r_t can be calculated from the b_2 and b_3 coefficients of the Gompertz equations, since $b_3 = -k_0^2/2$, and $b_2 = -k_0[(r_t/\beta) + 1]$. When $\beta = 0.15$ in (G2a), $k_0 = 0.81$, and $r_t = 6.7$ per cent, while for $\beta = 0.10$ in (G2b), $k_0 = 0.56$, and $r_t = 13.1$ per cent.

The post-school investment parameters cannot be identified in the parabolic equations unless values of T, the period of positive net investment, can be specified. Since T corresponds to the number of years of experience until earnings reach a plateau, $T = 20$ is used for annual earnings (P1) and $T = 30$ for weekly earnings (P3). In (P1) $k_0 = 0.58$ and $r_t = 6.3$ per cent, while in (P3), $k_0 = 0.42$ and $r_t = 11.9$ per cent.

In order to interpret the parameters of the earnings function in terms of gross investment and depreciation the Gompertz function is expanded to include a linear term in experience (equation 5.4g). This is shown in (G4). The coefficient of the linear term is an estimate of the depreciation rate δ ($= 1.2$ per cent). The estimate of initial gross investments k_0^* is 0.54, and the rate of return to post-school investment is estimated to be 12.1 per cent.

The high values of k_0 and low values of r_μ in (Gb) make the assumed rate of decline of investment, $\beta = 15$ per cent, somewhat less plausible than the alternative assumption of $\beta = 10$ per cent in (Ga).[8]

The parabolic gross investment formulation precludes the identification of the parameters: two need to be assumed to identify the remaining three.

5. Adding variation in weeks worked by (ln W) to the equation raises the explanatory power of the regressions to 52.5 per cent in the parabolic, and to 55.7 per cent in the Gompertz, equations. In both cases the coefficient at ln W is significantly larger than unity, suggesting a positive correlation between weeks worked and weekly earnings within schooling and experience levels.

Even without W, adding an (imperfect) experience term in the human capital earnings function raises its explanatory power from 7 per cent in the schooling regression to over 30 per cent in the Gompertz function while the bias in the estimated rate of return to schooling is largely eliminated. How well the regression coefficients of the ex-

---

8. All the estimates of k_0 seem rather high. The overstatement may be due to some confounding of investment with maturation effects, or with higher rates of return to post-school investment than to schooling.

perience variables estimate the post-school investment parameters is difficult to tell.

Firmer estimates will require more evidence. The rates of return to schooling are somewhat lower than they were in the overtaking set (Table 3.3). Possibly, these rates decline with experience in the cross section, as older cohorts have older vintages of schooling. The R^2 measures do not seem to be very sensitive to alternative specifications, and the R^2 are of major interest here.

While the expansion of the schooling model to a function which includes post-school experience greatly increases the power of the human capital analysis of earnings, our regressions still understate that power. Because there is no direct information on individual post-school investments, these were assumed to be the same for all persons within a schooling group. In effect, estimates were made of the contribution of individual investments in schooling measured in years, and of *average* post-school investments in each schooling group to total earnings inequality. This contribution amounts to about one-third of total inequality in annual earnings. The remainder contains effects of individual differences in post-school investments, in quality of schooling, in time supplied to the market or spent in unemployment, in individual rates of return, and in "transitory" factors. Because the first two are components of the volume of human capital investment, the regressions understate the potential explanatory power of the distribution of human capital investments.

How much larger would R^2 be if information were available on post-school investments for each individual? This question can be answered in an indirect fashion. Assume that the desired equation (5.6) which includes individual information on post-school investments is homoscedastic. Then $\sigma^2(u_i)$ is the same for all sets of values of the independent variables in equation (5.6):

$$\ln Y = \ln E_0 + rs_i + f_i(t) + u_i,$$

where $f_i(t)$ is the contribution of post-school investments to earnings. To estimate $\sigma^2(u_i)$, hence $\hat{R}^2 = 1 - [\sigma^2(u_i)/\sigma^2(\ln Y)]$, it is sufficient to estimate the residual variance in one instance only. This has already been done in the case where $f_i(t) = 0$, i.e., in the overtaking set. The residual variance in the regression of log earnings on schooling in that set serves, therefore, as an estimate of the residual variance in the unobservable regression form (5.6). Based on the regressions in the overtaking set, previously shown in Table 3.3, $\sigma^2(u) = 0.333$. Hence $\hat{R}^2 = 1 - (0.333/0.668) = 0.50$.

In a similar fashion, the residual variance from the multiple regression of log earnings on schooling and log weeks worked in the overtaking set can be compared to the aggregate variance of log earnings net of the contribution of log weeks. The resulting [9] $\hat{R}^2 = 1 - (0.20/0.53) = 0.62$.

If most of the variation in weeks worked were considered transitory, the 62 per cent figure would be an estimate of the contribution of human capital investment to a longer-run earnings inequality. If all of it were permanent and related to human capital investments, then $\hat{R}^2 = 1 - (0.200/0.668) = 0.70$.

In analyzing the regressions in the overtaking set I suggested that quality of schooling might account for at least 0.06 of the residual variance. If so, the indirect estimates $\hat{R}^2$ of the explanatory power of the distribution of human capital for the inequality of earnings increases to 0.55, 0.69, and 0.78, respectively.

It appears that, whatever the fraction of transitory variation in weeks worked, schooling and post-school investment accounted for close to two-thirds of the inequality of earnings of adult, white, urban men in the United States in 1959.

---

9. The residual variance in equation (2) in the top panel of Table 3.3 is 0.204; $0.53 = \sigma^2(\ln Y) - (1.142)^2\sigma^2(\ln W)$, where 1.142 is the coefficient in (G4) in Table 4.4.

6

Analysis of Residuals: Distributions of Earnings Within Schooling and Age Groups

6.1 VARIANCES

It was possible to make indirect estimates of the contribution of human capital investments to total earnings inequality by assuming that the latent residuals (u_i) in the earnings function (equation 5.6) were homoscedastic. Is this assumption consistent with the empirical data? This question is an invitation to explore the structure of earnings distributions within groups defined by years of schooling and years of age (experience). Since the within-group variation in earnings is quite large, such an exploration is of interest in its own right, and not merely as a test of particular assumptions.

The estimated values of the regression equations, which were shown in Table 5.1, are estimates of means in the schooling-experience groups. The within-group distributions are, therefore, distributions of residuals [1] (v_i) (equation 5.7). Since $v_i = u_i + (v_i - u_i)$,

$$\sigma^2(v_{it}) = \sigma^2(u_i) + \sigma^2(v_i - u_i) + 2\rho\sigma(u_i)\sigma(v_i - u_i).$$

---

1. Apart from the sampling errors of the means in each cell.

The observed residual variance $\sigma^2(v_i)$ in a schooling group changes over the life cycle (t) only if $\sigma^2(v_i - u_i)$ changes, assuming $\sigma^2(u_i)$ is homoscedastic and fixed.

By definition of equations (5.6) and (5.7) of Chapter 5, $v_i - u_i$ contains unobserved individual differences in returns to post-school investment. The human capital model (Chapter 2) predicts that the residual variance in a schooling group, $\sigma^2(v_i)$, will change systematically with age and experience.

6.1.1 EXPERIENCE PROFILES OF DOLLAR AND LOG VARIANCES OF EARNINGS

To analyze the experience profiles of both dollar variances $\sigma^2(Y_i)$ and log variances $\sigma^2(v_i) = \sigma^2(\ln Y_i)$, consider three points in the working life: the initial stage $t = 0$, the overtaking stage $t = \hat{j}$, and the peak earnings stage $t = t_p$. The arbitrariness and difficulty of deriving functional forms of profiles of variances is avoided by using this procedure, while making it possible to determine whether the profiles are monotonic.

First the expressions for dollar variances at the three points are derived:

$$Y_{si} = E_{si} - C_{0i}; \therefore \sigma^2(Y_s) = \sigma^2(E_{si}) + \sigma^2(C_0) - 2\rho_{C_0,E_s}\sigma(E_s)\sigma(C_0). \quad (6.1)$$

$$Y_{\hat{j}i} = E_{si}; \sigma^2(Y_{\hat{j}i}) = \sigma^2(E_s). \quad (6.2)$$

$$Y_{pi} = E_{si} + rC_T; \sigma^2(Y_p) = \sigma^2(E_s) + r^2\sigma^2(C_T) + 2r\rho_{C_T,E_s}\sigma(E_s)\sigma(C_T). \quad (6.3)$$

In each equation, C_0 is initial-period post-school investment; C_T, the sum of positive post-school net investments; E_s, initial post-school earning capacity; Y_p, peak earnings; ρ, correlation coefficient; and r, the rate of return to post-school investments.

In general, $\sigma^2(Y)$ must vary over the life cycle. The pattern of variation depends on the dispersion in post-school investments and on the correlation between the dollar volumes of post-school investment and earning capacity E_s. If, as appears from intergroup analysis (Chapter 2), the correlation between (dollar) schooling and post-school investment is positive, ρ is positive and dollar variances must rise from overtaking to peak earnings. In addition, dollar variances will rise throughout if $\sigma^2(Y_0) < \sigma^2(Y_{\hat{j}})$, which must be true if

$$\rho(C_0, E_s) > \frac{1}{2} \frac{\sigma(C_0)}{\sigma(E_s)}.$$

Chart 6.1 and Table 6.1 show that dollar variances indeed increase monotonically and sharply throughout working life. The standard deviations more than double between the eighth and thirtieth year of experience in the middle and upper schooling groups, but increase at a slower rate in the lower ones. The same data also show that the profiles of variances of the more educated are systematically higher at all stages of experience. A sufficient condition for this phenomenon can be found by comparing the variances at overtaking: Here $\sigma^2(Y_{\hat{j}}) = r_s^2 \sigma^2(C_s) + \sigma^2(u)$, when the variation in E_0 and r_s is impounded in the residual. $\sigma^2(C_s)$ evidently increases with level of schooling. This is quite plausible: over time, total costs of schooling cumulate with level of schooling, and so do individual differences in total costs.

The rate of growth of variances from $\hat{j}$ to t_p is obtained by dividing (6.2) into (6.3):

$$\frac{\sigma^2(Y_p)}{\sigma^2(Y_{\hat{j}})} - 1 = r^2 \frac{\sigma^2(C_T)}{\sigma^2(E_s)} + 2r\rho \frac{\sigma(C_T)}{\sigma(E_s)}. \tag{6.4}$$

The weaker growth of variances at lower levels of schooling suggests either a weaker correlation (ρ) between earnings capacity (E_s) and post-school investments (C_T), or a smaller ratio $\sigma(C_T)/\sigma(E_s)$. Define the regression slope of C_{Ti} on E_{si}, which is equal to $\rho[\sigma(C_T)/\sigma(E_s)]$ as the "marginal propensity to invest" (MPI). Evidently, MPI tends to be smaller at lower levels of schooling.[2]

The important conclusion resulting from the analysis of dollar variances is that the usually observed increases of variances with experience and age are strongly influenced by the staggering of post-school investments over individual working lives. A large enough dispersion of post-school investments and a positive correlation between dollar schooling and post-school investments can explain the sharp age gradients. The increases of dollar variances with education are likely to reflect the almost necessarily larger residual dollar dispersion of total schooling costs at higher levels of schooling.

---

2. Cf. the findings of Solmon (1972) that the marginal propensity to save is also smaller at lower levels of schooling.

CHART 6.1
EXPERIENCE PROFILES OF VARIANCES OF ANNUAL EARNINGS OF
WHITE, NONFARM MEN, 1959

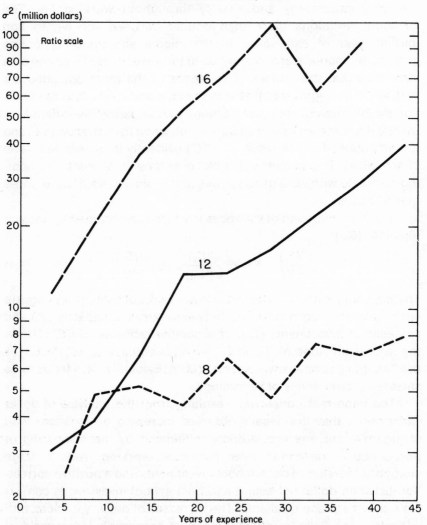

NOTE: Figures on curves indicate years of schooling completed.
SOURCE: 1/1,000 sample of U.S. Census, 1960.

TABLE 6.1
AGE PROFILES OF DISPERSION IN EARNINGS, 1959
(white, nonfarm men)

	Years of Schooling					
	5–8	12	16	5–8	12	16
Age	Standard Deviation			Variance of Logs		
	Annual Earnings					
20–24	$2,200	$1,730	($ 2,360)	.562	.454	–
25–29	2,280	1,970	3,270	.457	.258	.360
30–34	2,110	2,590	4,530	.336	.231	.251
35–39	2,570	3,650	6,040	.358	.240	.317
40–44	2,200	3,680	7,340	.371	.272	.421
45–49	2,730	4,070	8,590	.360	.339	.555
50–54	2,620	4,710	10,550	.392	.403	.626
55–59	2,820	5,390	8,920	.424	.451	.612
60–64	3,360	6,340	9,700	.525	.460	.933
	Weekly Earnings					
20–24	$53.3	$ 46.3	$ 46.1	.489	.363	–
25–29	47.1	39.0	70.6	.320	.205	.235
30–34	44.7	46.0	75.1	.263	.183	.212
35–39	43.3	65.0	102.2	.266	.203	.277
40–44	46.0	69.0	121.7	.275	.226	.336
45–49	56.2	77.1	144.4	.310	.270	.424
50–54	53.2	82.3	176.6	.292	.312	.436
55–59	55.1	93.0	153.3	.328	.317	.552
60–64	63.3	107.8	162.8	.409	.369	.748

SOURCE: 1/1,000 sample of U.S. Census, 1960.

A positive correlation between means and variances of economic variables is a frequently encountered empirical phenomenon. It might be taken for granted as an arithmetical necessity, which it is not. The structure of means and variances of earnings in these schooling-age cells is an example of it. In this case, however, the human capital model provides an explanation: higher levels of earnings represent returns cumulated by additional investment. Thus if H_1 is a lower stock of human capital and $H_2 = H_1 + \Delta H$ is a higher one, earnings $E_1 = rH_1$ and $E_2 = r(H_1 + \Delta H)$. Then $E_2 > E_1$ and $\sigma^2(E_2) >$

$\sigma^2(E_1)$ so long as the correlation between H_1 and ΔH is not excessively negative. Indeed, a positive correlation is expected, since the determinants of investment in current and past periods are likely to persist for a given individual.

6.1.2 ANALYSIS OF MARGINAL VARIANCES OF EARNINGS

Dollar standard deviations of earnings in marginal distributions, that is, in distributions of all earnings in a given row or column of the two-way classification of the population by schooling and experience (or age), are shown in Table 6.3, column 2, below. The total variance in such a group (say an age group) is, by (2.12):

$$\sigma_T^2 = \frac{1}{n} \sum_{i=1}^{s} n_i(\sigma_i^2 + d_i^2), \tag{6.5}$$

where n is the number of observations in the age group; n_i, the number of observations in the ith schooling cell; σ_i^2, the within-cell variance; and $d_i = (\bar{X}_i - \bar{X}_a)$, the differential between the mean in the cell and the overall mean of the age group.

Clearly, marginal variances σ_T^2 (therefore, standard deviations) must increase with experience and with age, because within-cell variances σ_i^2 increase, and because d_i, differentials among profiles of means, also increase, as we learned in Chapter 4. The increase of σ_T^2 is sharper in age groups than in experience groups, because the intergroup differential d_i grows more rapidly in the former: age profiles of mean earnings diverge more strongly than experience profiles.

Similarly, variances in the marginal distributions by schooling must increase with schooling, again because cell variances σ_i^2 and mean age differentials d_i increase with schooling.

These statements are based on the assumption that the relative frequencies n_i/N are the same in each marginal row or column, that is, the age distributions are the same in all schooling groups, and the schooling distribution is the same in all age groups. This would be the case in a cohort which is followed over its working life, or in the cross section if there were no secular trends in schooling. The effect of such secular trends is, of course, that the weights n_i/N differ systematically in the cross section: they are bigger in older age cells at lower levels of schooling, and in higher schooling cells at younger ages. For this reason the age increases in marginal variances are likely to be less in the cross sections than in cohorts. In the cross-sectional age comparisons, there is, however, an offsetting effect due to secular trends in the dispersion of schooling. Whatever the difference from cohorts, the cross-sectional gradients are quite strong, as shown in Table 6.3, below.

6.1.3 ANALYSIS OF LOG VARIANCES OF EARNINGS

We now turn to a similar analysis of relative variances, $\sigma^2(\ln Y_i)$, in groupings of the earnings distribution. The observations are shown in Table 6.1 and in Charts 6.2–6.4. Again, consider three points in the working life:

$$\ln Y_{si} = \ln E_{si} + \ln (1 - k_{0i}); \tag{6.6}$$

$$\therefore \sigma^2(\ln Y_s) = \sigma^2(\ln E_s) + \sigma^2 \ln (1 - k_0) + 2\rho_1\sigma(\ln E_s)\sigma \ln (1 - k_0).$$

$$\ln Y_{ji} = \ln E_{si}; \; \sigma^2(\ln Y_j) = \sigma^2(\ln E_s). \tag{6.7}$$

$$\ln Y_{pi} = \ln E_{si} + rK_{Ti}; \; \sigma^2(\ln Y_p)$$

$$= \sigma^2(\ln E_s) + r^2\sigma^2(K_T) + 2\rho_2 r\sigma(\ln E_s)\sigma(K_T). \tag{6.8}$$

Now, the change in log variances over the working life depends on the size of the dispersion in cumulated post-school investments ratios K_T and on the correlation between $\ln E_s(= \ln E_0 + rs)$ and K_T. A positive correlation between time-equivalent post-school investment K_T and initial post-school earning capacity $\ln E_s$ implies a negative correlation between $\ln E_s$ and $\ln (1 - k_0)$. If the correlations are weak, $\rho_2 = \rho_1 = 0$ and the profile of log variances is U-shaped, with the bottom at overtaking. The U-shape is preserved if the correlations are within a specified interval bracketing zero.[3] A more pronounced negative value of ρ_2 implies a monotonic decline in log variances over the working life, while a stronger positive ρ_2 implies a monotonic growth in log variances.

A zero correlation between the investment ratio and initial post-

---

3. The intervals are $|\rho_1| < \dfrac{1}{2} \dfrac{\sigma[\ln (1 - k_0)]}{\sigma(\ln E_s)}$, and $|\rho_2| < \dfrac{1}{2} \dfrac{\sigma(K)}{\sigma(\ln E_s)}$.

CHART 6.2
EXPERIENCE PROFILES OF LOG VARIANCES OF ANNUAL EARNINGS
OF WHITE, NONFARM MEN, 1959

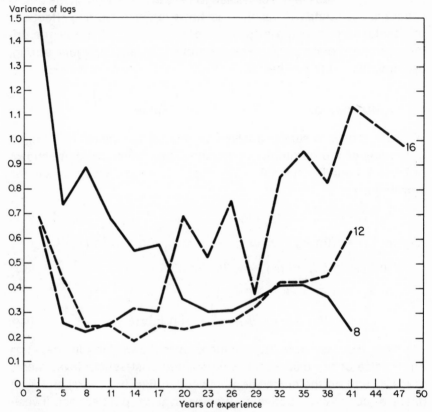

Variance of logs

Years of experience

NOTE: Figures on curves indicate years of schooling completed.
SOURCE: 1/1,000 sample of U.S. Census, 1960.

school earning capacity may be due to a unitary elasticity of dollar
post-school investment with respect to initial earning capacity.
Positive correlations may be caused by elasticities above 1; negative
correlations, by elasticities below 1. Charts 6.2 and 6.3 indicate that
experience profiles of log variances are largely U-shaped in the central (12 years) schooling groups, suggesting a weak correlation
between post-school investment ratios and earning capacity within
this schooling level; tend to be positively inclined (show pronounced
growth) in the upper schooling groups, suggesting a positive correlation; and are negatively inclined (decline, by and large) at lower

CHART 6.3

Experience Profiles of Log Variances of Annual Earnings of White, Nonfarm Men Working Year-round, 1959

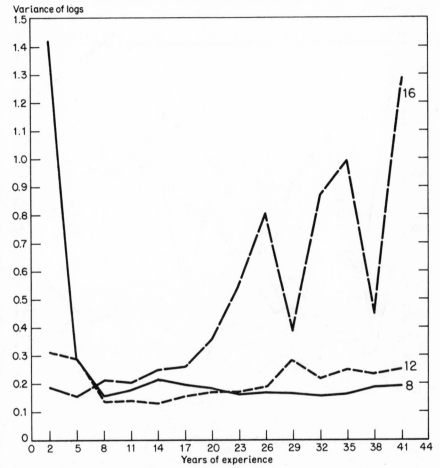

Variance of logs

Years of experience

Note: Figures on curves indicate years of schooling completed.
Source: 1/1,000 sample of U.S. Census, 1960.

levels, suggesting a negative correlation.[4] Apparently, the within-group elasticity of post-school investment is a positive function of schooling. This finding is formally consistent with the other findings:

4. The stronger growth of both dollar and relative variances at higher than at lower levels of skill (occupation or education) was noted in different data by several analysts. Cf. Adams (1958), Hill (1959), Lydall (1968), Mincer (1957), and Morgan et al. (1962).

CHART 6.4

PROFILES OF RELATIVE SKEWNESS OF ANNUAL EARNINGS OF WHITE, NONFARM
MEN, 1959

NOTE: Figures on curves indicate years of schooling completed.
SOURCE: 1/1,000 sample of U.S. Census, 1960.

The ratio k_t is an "average propensity to invest." According to the analysis of log-experience profiles of mean earnings in Table 4.1, it tends to decline from lower to higher schooling groups. At the same time, the profiles of dollar variances suggest that the "marginal propensity to invest" increases with the level of schooling. Elasticities, therefore, increase correspondingly and more strongly.

Another explanation of the difference in log-variance profiles among schooling groups may be found in the serial correlations of investments (the correlation between C_T and E_s is an example of it). Less stability in investment (and in employment) behavior over the life cycle results in weaker growth of variances at lower levels of schooling. It is also possible, as we noted before, that the mean earnings profile overstates the size of post-school investments in the lower schooling groups. If so, the dispersion of post-school investments is likely to be a less important component in explaining patterns of earnings inequality at lower than at middle and higher levels of schooling.[5]

While dollar variances were larger at higher schooling levels at overtaking, with the plausible interpretation that $\sigma^2(C_s)$ increases with schooling, no comparable statement can be made a priori about $\sigma^2(s)$, unless the ranking of the variation in schooling quality were known. The observed log variances (Chart 6.3) indeed differ very little among schooling groups below college at that stage in the distribution of full-time earnings. Relative (time equivalent) variation in college quality evidently exceeds that at lower levels of schooling. In all earnings (Chart 6.2), variances of the schooling groups below high school are inflated, an effect of large variation of weeks worked during the year (cf. Chapter 7). Because the differently inclined profiles of variances intersect in the second decade of experience, there is a reversal of ranking in inequality by level of schooling: inverse at first and direct in the later parts of the working life. This pattern is not changed much by shifting from the experience comparisons to comparisons based on age.

It is easy to see that these configurations, together with the structure of mean log-earnings profiles, produce U-shaped patterns of *marginal* relative variances by age. These are shown in Table 6.3, column 1. The strong growth of mean differentials d_i with age contributes to the stronger age gradient of inequality and to the earlier reversal of it by age than by experience. In published empirical research, this reversal was noted as a persistent feature of relative earnings structures.[6]

The distinction between cross-sectional and cohort patterns of

---

5. Some evidence on the particular importance of the variation in weeks worked at lower levels of schooling is seen in the comparison of Charts 6.2 and 6.3 and in Table 7.2, below.

6. Cf. Morgan (1962).

marginal relative variances can be analyzed by means of equation 6.5, above, as were the dollar variances. The implications are similar, except that because of differences in the numbers included in the old and young age groupings within schooling groups, the cross-sectional relation of inequality to schooling has a more negative tilt than that in the cohort, though still somewhat U-shaped, as Table 6.3, column 1, indicates.

Since the purpose of this study was to relate the structure and inequality in the distribution of earnings to the distribution of *amounts* invested in human capital, individual variation in rates of return was ignored. However, in studying the patterns of residuals v_i, variation in rates of return cannot be entirely ignored. But a hypothesis that the observed residual variances contain mainly variation in rates of return rather than variation in post-school investment can be rejected. It was shown, in Part I, that the assumptions $\sigma^2(r) > 0$, while $\sigma^2(C_T) = 0$, leads to a monotonic increase in the residual dollar variances over working life, provided $C_T > 0$. However, $\sigma^2(C_T) = 0$ means that the same dollar amount is invested by each individual, so K_T, the investment ratio, is perfectly negatively correlated with earnings E_s. But that would produce sharp monotonic *decreases* in log variances over the life cycle. The empirical evidence contradicts such a hypothesis.

The hypothesis that $\sigma^2(r) > 0$ and $\sigma^2(k_t) = 0$, while $k_t > 0$, means that there is a perfect positive correlation between C_t and E_s. However, the strong decay of the correlation between schooling and earnings shown in Table 3.4 (Chapter 3) contradicts this hypothesis.

I conclude that post-school investment varies among persons with the same schooling both in dollars and in time-equivalents. The variation in rates of return has no effect on the profiles of residual variances, unless there is post-school investment and it has a non-zero variance. Indeed, the latter is a sufficient explanation of the profiles of residual variance shown in Charts 6.1–6.3. This, of course, does not deny the existence of dispersion in rates of return.[7]

The negative ranking of inequality with respect to schooling seen in the profiles of relative variance in the earlier stages of working life and the reverse ranking later are in no obvious way related to

---

7. Indeed, as I argued in Chapter 1, post-school investment has no effect on the distribution of earnings in the overtaking set. Hence the residual variance in that distribution, after correction for schooling quality and weeks worked, can be interpreted as resulting from individual variation in rates of return.

secular trends in human capital, such as the upward trend in schooling. The presence of these trends does affect our understanding of the cross section, as we noticed, only when we aggregate the two-way groupings (age *and* schooling) into marginal, that is, one-way groups (age *or* schooling). Because of these trends, higher schooling groups are more prevalent at younger ages, and conversely. In aggregating cross sections, therefore, parameters of the more educated groups receive greater weight in the younger age groups, and those of the less educated receive greater weight in the older ones. Given the reversal of profiles of inequality, therefore, the stronger the upward trend in schooling, the greater the attenuation of aggregate inequality, as larger weights are attached to the smaller relative variances. Or, to put it differently, if there were no trends in schooling, and the distribution of schooling in each age group were the same as the currently observed distribution among all earners, regardless of age, aggregate inequality would be larger than currently observed. The hypothetical distribution would, in effect, be a distribution over the working life of a fixed cohort. A simulation experiment utilizing 13×9 experience parameters and frequencies of schooling groups shows that, under these assumptions, the aggregate log variance in the cohort, that is, in the trendless cross section, would be 0.805 compared to 0.668. Thus the growth of schooling reduces the aggregate inequality observed in the cross section by about 17 per cent, and this effect is obtained not by narrowing the distribution of schooling but by diminishing the importance of groups whose post-school behavior generates a great deal of dispersion in earnings.

The same experiment which keeps the distribution of schooling in each experience group the same as at overtaking ($j = 7$–9 years) yields an aggregate variance of logs of 0.721. This is an estimate of the inequality in the cohort which was at overtaking in 1959. The fraction of aggregate inequality attributable to human capital investment based on this figure is an estimate which abstracts from secular trends in schooling. It is a few percentage points higher than the estimates based on the observed cross section.

6.2   SHAPES OF RESIDUAL DISTRIBUTIONS

Shapes of the within-group earnings distributions are portrayed in Chart 6.4, which shows experience profiles of asymmetry (relative

TABLE 6.2
AGE PROFILES OF SKEWNESS IN EARNINGS, 1959
(white, nonfarm men)

	Years of Schooling					
	5–8	12	16	5–8	12	16
Age	Bowley's Coefficient			Ratio: Mean to Median		
20–24	.107	.039	.232	1.100	1.015	1.178
25–29	−.009	−.025	.119	1.046	1.002	1.101
30–34	.077	.154	.281	1.043	1.045	1.167
35–39	−.028	.211	.256	1.028	1.095	1.121
40–44	−.078	.180	.362	1.022	1.100	1.200
45–49	.057	.222	.463	1.035	1.131	1.182
50–54	.017	.200	.527	1.023	1.132	1.271
55–59	.074	.252	.328	1.049	1.173	1.220
60–64	−.005	.295	.584	1.051	1.238	1.410

SOURCE: 1/1,000 sample of U.S. Census, 1960.

skewness) of earnings in each of the schooling groups. The measure of skewness is Bowley's coefficient:

$$RSk = \frac{(P_{90} - Md) - (Md - P_{10})}{P_{90} - P_{10}},$$

where P denotes percentile and Md median of the distribution. Quite similar results are obtained when the ratio of mean to median is used as a measure of skewness (Table 6.2).

Skewness grows montonically in the upper schooling groups, its profile is U-shaped in the high-school group, and it first rapidly declines and then levels off in the lowest group. Its ranking is directly related to schooling level, except during the first decade of experience, when the ranking is inverse. The pattern resembles the profiles of log variances and can be interpreted in much the same fashion: A strong positive correlation between investment ratios k_{ti} and earning capacities E_{si} within higher levels of schooling, a weak correlation in the middle, and a negative correlation at the lower levels of schooling.

The similarity of the behavior of skewness measured by the mean-to-median ratio and of the log variances is theoretically assured when the distributions are log-normal.[8] More generally, consider the experience profile of gross earnings: $E_{t+1} = E_t(1 + rk_t)$.

By a theorem of C. C. Craig (1936), the distribution E_{t+1} is more positively (less negatively) skewed than the distribution of E_t, if the correlation between E_t and k_t is zero or positive. During the first period of observed earnings, $Y_{s0} = E_s(1 - k_0)$. If the correlation of k_t with E_t is strongly positive, so is that of k_0 with E_s. In that case, skewness of initial earnings (Y_{s0}) is likely to be smaller than at overtaking (E_s). The U-shaped result of a near-zero correlation, and a declining profile of skewness due to a negative correlation are deduced in the same way.

The association between schooling and skewness, at given stages of experience, appears positive more often than the association between schooling and inequality (log variance), since the reversal of ranks takes place earlier in the working life (Chart 6.4). This is partly because the greater incidence of employment instability reduces positive skewness at lower levels of schooling.[9] In consequence, in the marginal distributions skewness generally increases with age and with schooling (see Table 6.3). This is not only because within-group skewness is larger at higher schooling levels and older ages. As noted before, in the aggregation process, the positive correlation between group variances and group means augments skewness and sharpens the gradient.

Positive skewness is a persistent feature of aggregate income distributions. Its presence has drawn a great deal of attention, starting with Pareto. Many of the theories of income distribution,[10] particularly the stochastic models, which will be discussed in the next section, were concentrated almost exclusively on this feature of the distribution. As we have seen, in human capital models, skewness is analyzed and explained at several levels. In the schooling model, skewness is made conditional on the shape of the distribution of schooling, and is not predicted as an inherent and persistent feature: the shape of the schooling distribution is exogenous to the model and does change secularly. Already the schooling distributions of the younger cohorts in the United States are negatively skewed. Why then does positive skewness persist?

---

8. See Aitchison and Brown (1957, pp. 22–23).
9. See discussion section 7.2.
10. Cf. Mincer (1970).

TABLE 6.3
INEQUALITY AND SKEWNESS IN MARGINAL DISTRIBUTIONS
OF EARNINGS, 1959
(white, nonfarm men)

	Log Variance (1)	Dollar Standard Deviation (2)	Skewness		
			Logs [a] (3)	Dollars [a] (4)	RM [b] (5)
Age					
25–29	.433	2,610⎱	⎰	⎱−.020	1.015
30–34	.343	3,060⎰ −.206		⎰ .140	1.068
35–39	.388	4,050⎱	⎱	⎱.157	1.107
40–44	.426	4,380⎰ −.131		⎰.167	1.119
45–49	.498	4,880⎱	⎱	⎱.172	1.163
50–54	.506	5,180⎰ −.151		⎰.190	1.174
55–59	.590	4,620⎱	⎱	⎱.176	1.162
60–64	.671	5,490⎰ −.193		⎰.185	1.188
Schooling (years)					
Under 8	.740	2,120		.018	1.070
8	.682	3,020	−.350	.066	1.057
9–11	.542	3,280		.128	1.072
12	.397	3,740	−.242	.178	1.111
13–15	.503	5,160		.349	1.211
16 or more	.534	6,810	+.046	.440	1.314

a. Bowley's measure of skewness.
b. Ratio of mean to median.

The answer lies in the positive correlation between dollar means and variances in the age-schooling groups of the earnings structure. As was pointed out before, this correlation reflects persistence in human capital accumulation: individuals who accumulate more capital over a lifetime invest larger amounts in most of the successive time periods.

Some of the stochastic or mathematical theories of income distribution generate Pareto or log-normal "equilibrium" distributions. Both forms are positively skewed. The Pareto distribution is also positively skewed in logs, while the log-normal one is symmetric in logs. Observed distributions, however, are typically positively skewed in dollars and *negatively* skewed in logs (Table 6.3, column 3).[11]

11. See also the findings of T. P. Hill (1959).

In the 1959 earnings data, the dollar distribution of earnings at overtaking was practically symmetric. It was, therefore, negatively skewed in logs, as was the distribution of schooling in years. Since dollar skewness grows with experience and age, logarithmic negative skewness diminishes correspondingly, as is shown in Table 6.3, column 3.

It also appears from the analysis of profiles of relative variances (Charts 6.2 and 6.3) that the sign of the overall correlation between group means and variances in logs is neither clearly positive nor negative: Group variances are positively related to means at upper levels of schooling and experience, negatively at lower levels. There is, therefore, little reason for the aggregation process to produce positive skewness or symmetry in logs in the overall distribution, when this is not true of the components. There is an implication, however, that aggregation within upper schooling-experience groups, hence upper earnings groups, tends to impart positive logarithmic skewness, while aggregation within lower earnings groups does the opposite. This may well explain the leptokurtic shape of the overall distribution, which has been observed in a number of studies (Rutherford, 1955; Bjerke, 1969; Lydall, 1968). When drawn on log-normal probability paper, the graph of the cumulative distribution is S-shaped, strongly concave at lower levels of earnings, and convex at upper levels. This reflects strong negative skewness (in logs) at lower levels and some positive skewness at upper levels of earnings. When drawn on normal probability paper, the lower level of the graph is linear (zero dollar skewness), the upper sharply convex (strong positive skewness in dollars). Chart 6.5 shows that the graph of a component distribution at a lower age-schooling group shows a relatively good fit to the normal distribution, while the graph of a higher age-schooling group shows a closer fit to the log-normal.

Summing up: If earnings distributions are to be classified on a scale of skewness somewhere between normal distributions (zero dollar skewness), log-normal (zero log skewness), and Pareto (positive log skewness), they fit between the normal and log-normal. As indicated by the curves in Chart 6.5, shapes of component distributions when ranked by average level of human capital systematically range from symmetry in dollars to symmetry in logarithms. This is entirely consistent with the theoretical conjecture in Chapter 2.

CHART 6.5
FIT OF ANNUAL EARNINGS DISTRIBUTIONS TO NORMAL AND LOG-NORMAL CURVES, 1959
(white, nonfarm men)

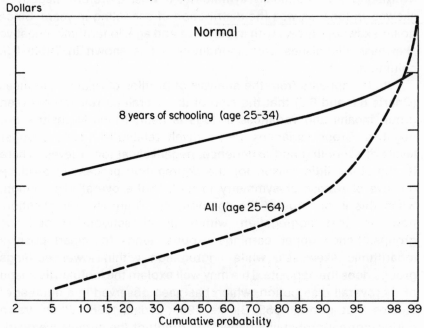

Dollars

Normal

8 years of schooling (age 25-34)

All (age 25-64)

2   5   10 15 20   30 40 50 60 70   80 85 90   95   98 99
Cumulative probability

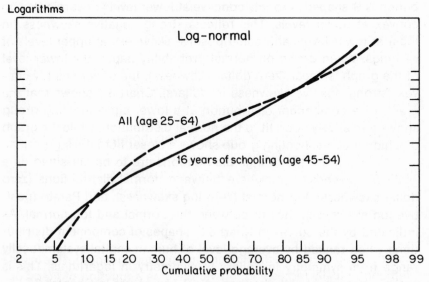

Logarithms

Log-normal

All (age 25-64)

16 years of schooling (age 45-54)

2   5   10 15 20   30 40 50 60 70   80 85 90   95   98 99
Cumulative probability

NOTE: Figures on each curve show age (in parentheses) and years of schooling completed.

SOURCE: 1/1,000 sample of U.S. Census, 1960.

114

7

Random Shock, Employment Variation, and Aggregation

7.1   HUMAN CAPITAL VERSUS RANDOM SHOCK MODELS

According to the foregoing analysis, the "residual," that is, within-group variation in earnings can be attributed to individual variation in returns to post-school investment, in rates of return, in quality of schooling, and to a variety of other factors which may be lumped together as the "unexplained" or, rather, "unmeasured" component ϵ_i (equation 5.5).

In stochastic theories of income distribution ϵ_i is interpreted as year-to-year individual fluctuation in earnings and the whole structure of earnings is explained by a stochastic process that is attributed to this "random shock" ϵ_i. These models specify that:

$$v_i = \ln Y_i = \ln Y_0 + \sum_{j=1}^{t} \epsilon_j,$$

where the ϵ_j are homoscedastic and mutually independent. This leads to a monotonically increasing log variance as a function of t (age or experience), and a positively skewed aggregate distribution (log-normal or Pareto, depending on differences in assumptions). But, as we have seen, the prediction that logarithmic variances of income grow monotonically and equally in all skill (schooling) groups is largely incorrect.

The greater and richer explanatory power of the human capital model need not preclude some validity in the random shock approach. Moreover, some of the predictions are similar: log variances of earnings do grow in some schooling groups and over certain phases of the working life. Even so, the same empirical phenomena are differently interpreted in the two models. In the stochastic models temporal variation in income is interpreted as chance variation. In contrast, in human capital models, much of the temporal variation in earnings is viewed as a systematic and persistent consequence of cumulative investment behavior. Discrimination between the two views can be sought in so-called panel correlations of earnings of the same cohort in two different time periods.

If we follow the earnings experience of a cohort m years after the initial year t, the random shock model implies that: (1) log variances will increase by the same amount $\sigma^2(\epsilon)$ each year, so that:

$$\sigma^2(\ln Y_{t+m}) = \sigma^2(\ln Y_t) + m\sigma^2(\epsilon); \qquad (7.1)$$

and (2) panel correlations, that is, correlations between $\ln Y_t$ and $\ln Y_{t+m}$, will decay continuously as the interval m is widened:

$$R^2(\ln Y_t, \ln Y_{t+m}) = \frac{\sigma^2(\ln Y_t)}{\sigma^2(\ln Y_{t+m})}, \qquad (7.2)$$

and

$$\frac{1}{R^2} = 1 + m\left[\frac{\sigma^2(\epsilon)}{\sigma^2(\ln Y_t)}\right]. \qquad (7.3)$$

According to the random shock model, both variances and the reciprocals of the coefficients of determination should increase linearly with the time interval m. We have already seen (Charts 6.2 and 6.3) a contradiction in that the profiles of variances are not linear. If it could be assumed that the profiles are linear, the steeper slope at the higher schooling level (Charts 6.2 and 6.3) implies a greater importance of random shock there, that is, a larger $\sigma^2(\epsilon)$, hence a more rapid decay of panel correlations in the higher schooling groups (since $\sigma^2(\epsilon)/\sigma^2(\ln Y_t)$ would be larger at higher schooling levels). Again, this implication is not substantiated in Table 7.1,

TABLE 7.1
Panel Correlations of Male Earnings, Based on Consumers Union Panel, 1959 Survey

Initial Year (t)	12 or Less			13–15			16			17 or More			All		
	2	7	11	2	7	11	2	7	11	2	7	11	2	7	11
							Coefficients of Determination (R^2)								
4	.989	.227	.312	.911	.444	.518	.854	.302	.376	.803	.441	.316	.822	.388	.430
7	.951	.220	.268	.852	.324	.265	.691	.383	.381	.760	.430	.388	.752	.426	.348
9	.711	.491	.279	.800	.396	.483	.712	.598	.527	.800	.461	.381	.785	.503	.453
12	.837	.654	.498	.907	.648	.616	.889	.581	.552	.897	.528	.679	.878	.578	.586
15	.846	.520	.412	.816	.684	.507	.932	.538	.615	.873	.555	.608	.824	.630	.608
18	.818	.588	.399	.898	.604	.591	.918	.652	.662	.887	.652	.739	.898	.681	.714
21	.899	.483	.498	.839	.699	.643	.874	.771	.755	.925	.771	.596	.871	.716	.658
24	.828	.419	.403	.931	.764	.688	.966	.768	.715	.908	.868	.637	.930	.788	.648
27	.902	.682	.744	.935	.801	.860	.955	.765	.757	.982	.794	.419	.952	.793	.781
Average	.864	.476	.423	.876	.596	.574	.865	.595	.593	.870	.611	.529	.856	.611	.580
							Reciprocals of R^2								
Average of															
t = 4, 7	1.031	4.475	3.468	1.135	2.669	2.852	1.308	2.960	2.641	1.280	2.301	2.872	1.272	2.462	2.598
All	1.165	2.451	2.588	1.143	1.834	1.914	1.170	1.845	1.896	1.155	1.744	2.051	1.172	1.735	1.833
t = 12	1.170	1.845	2.129	1.129	1.440	1.576	1.085	1.503	1.498	1.097	1.505	1.683	1.128	1.451	1.515

NOTE: Earnings at t years of experience are correlated with earnings at $t + m$ years of experience; $t + m$ is in 1959 for each of the cohorts; $m = 2$, 7, or 11, as indicated in the column headings.

which is based on a 1959 survey of the Consumers Union Panel,[1] and contains panel correlations (R^2) and their inverses ($1/R^2$). Data on past earnings from which the correlations were calculated are based on recall of respondents. Recall data probably contain a great deal of error, which may affect the level and pattern of the coefficients of determination. In an attempt to minimize this error, correlations of earnings at t and $t + m$ years of experience were observed only in those cohorts whose experience did not exceed $t + m$. Thus, only rows in Table 7.1 pertain to given cohorts. Years of experience were provided by respondents as time elapsed since they first entered full-time employment.

Despite the unpredictable effects of errors in such data, there are two features in the table that are noteworthy: (1) As the interval m is widened from two to seven years, the correlation declines sharply when the panel base t is in the first decade of experience. The decline is much milder thereafter. (2) When the interval m is widened further, from seven to eleven years, the decline in correlation, if any, is negligible. The growth in $1/R^2$ is not linear, particularly over the earlier decades of experience. These findings are clearly inconsistent with the random shock model. They do seem reasonable in the light of the human capital model: panel correlations bracketing the overtaking stage would be expected to be relatively weak, but stronger thereafter.[2] The sharp deceleration or even halt in the decline of correlations beyond a seven-year span is not implausible: beyond overtaking, the ranking of individual earnings acquires a long-run stability, though disturbed by short-run, "transitory" fluctuations.

The panel correlations are consistent with a human capital model

---

1. There were 4,191 usable responses in the recall data. Over half of the respondents were college graduates. For a detailed description of the data, see Juster (1964).

2. When the interval brackets the overtaking point, we are correlating

$$\ln E_s + \sum_{j=0}^{t-1} (rk_j - k_t)$$

with

$$\ln E_s + \sum_{j=1}^{t+m-1} (rk_j - k_{t+m}).$$

By definition, the post-school investment component of earnings is negative before overtaking and positive thereafter. The bracketing, therefore, introduces a negative correlation between the investment components of earnings, which weakens the panel correlation. Indeed, if $\sigma^2(\ln E_s)$ were zero, this correlation would be negative.

in which post-school investments and their ratios to earnings vary among individuals $[\sigma^2(k_t) > 0]$. In a model in which this variation is de-emphasized but the variation in rates of return is stressed instead $[\sigma^2(r) > 0]$, the implicit panel correlations would be high and independent of either the span of the panel interval m or the stage in the working life. Since the current-investment component is, in that case, constant for all individuals, panel correlations of net earnings would be the same as panel correlations of gross earnings. It is precisely the difference between net and gross earnings that creates some of the indicated features of the observed panel correlations.

7.2   VARIATION IN EMPLOYMENT AS A FACTOR IN EARNINGS INEQUALITY

The finding that systematic investment components account for a large part of the temporal and individual variation in earnings does not preclude the existence of a random component ϵ_i: panel correlations are certainly less than unity. But even a modest random component need not have the stochastic properties specified in the random shock models. Instead of being independent of the previous level of income, thereby creating an explosive variance, the random "transitory" component may be unrelated to a latent "permanent" level of income, so that the variance does not change much over time, if at all. Under this formulation, introduced by Friedman (1957), the contribution of the "transitory" component to total income inequality was estimated from income and consumption data to be about 20–30 per cent. This fraction is probably somewhat smaller in earnings than in total income,[3] and roughly compares in size to my estimates of the separate contributions of age variation and employment variation to total earnings inequality. The size of the log variance of earnings at the overtaking stage of the life cycle is about 25 per cent smaller than the aggregate variance, which may be viewed as a rough estimate of the contribution of age variation to total inequality. The contribution of employment variation, according to the regressions in Table 5.1, was also nearly one-fourth of total inequality.

---

3. "Transitory" variation in property and self-employment income is likely to be more pronounced than in earnings.

Which of the two factors should be considered transitory? Their joint contribution greatly exceeds the contribution of "transitories" as estimated from consumption data. The answer is that not all of the age variation can be considered transitory in the sense used in consumption studies: the consumption "horizon"[4] is short relative to the full length of the earnings profile. Similarly, not all of the employment variation, such as in weeks worked during the year, is transitory: some persons usually work less than others, some regularly experience greater turnover and unemployment than others.

Some of the "permanent" variation in weeks worked is an effect of human capital investments: larger investments by workers and employers tend to reduce worker turnover and unemployment (Becker, 1964, p. 18 ff.). Moreover, increased wages resulting from human capital investments may affect the labor supply. In either case, to the extent that employment during the year is an *effect* of human capital investments, and not an independent factor, the contribution of employment variation to earnings inequality should be credited to the distribution of human capital.

The theory of specific human capital (Becker, 1964) predicts an inverse relation between employment stability and the quantity of investment.[5] Assuming a positive correlation between specific and total post-school investments, as well as between schooling and job training—all measured in dollar costs—the empirical prediction is of a positive relation between schooling or age and the mean number of weeks worked in a group, as well as a negative relation between schooling or age and the standard deviation of weeks worked in the group. Table 7.2 shows that these relations do hold.

The fact that weeks worked and their dispersion are inversely associated across schooling and age groups[6] suggests that the employment factor represents a force in the direction of negative skewness of earnings. The incidence of underemployment is strongest at the lower levels of skill—a fact consistent with human capital theory. Yet for earnings distributions the employment implications of human

---

4. The "planning horizon" of the consumer may be measured by the inverse of the consumer discount rate.

5. Human capital investment is specific to a firm to the extent that it increases the marginal productivity of workers in the firm more than in other firms.

6. This negative correlation of means with variances produces negative skewness of the aggregate distribution of weeks worked.

TABLE 7.2
Weeks Worked in 1959, by Age and Schooling
(white, nonfarm men)

	Years of Schooling								
	5–8			12			16		
Age	$\overline{W}$	$\sigma(W)$	$\dfrac{\sigma^2(W)}{\sigma^2(\ln Y)}$	$\overline{W}$	$\sigma(W)$	$\dfrac{\sigma^2(W)}{\sigma^2(\ln Y)}$	$\overline{W}$	$\sigma(W)$	$\dfrac{\sigma^2(W)}{\sigma^2(\ln Y)}$
20–24	43.5	.288	.692	45.0	.209	.518			
25–29	44.2	.218	.485	48.4	.130	.333	46.9	.158	.368
30–34	45.7	.179	.432	49.0	.105	.250	49.7	.074	.104
35–39	45.9	.175	.397	49.0	.099	.200	40.6	.081	.117
40–44	46.3	.175	.383	49.3	.125	.308	50.3	.074	.078
45–49	46.0	.173	.353	48.7	.128	.250	49.8	.097	.076
50–54	45.9	.168	.329	48.5	.133	.237	49.5	.093	.086
55–59	45.6	.195	.413	48.5	.117	.165	49.0	.056	.026
60–64	44.8	.232	.509	47.7	.129	.195	48.2	.143	.114

$\overline{W}$ = mean number of weeks.
$\sigma(W)$ = standard deviation of (logs of) weeks.
$\sigma^2(W)/\sigma^2(\ln Y)$ = ratio of variance of weeks to variance of earnings (in logs).

capital theory are the exact opposite of the direct productivity implications of the same theory. The latter produce a positive correlation between means and variances of subgroups, the former a negative correlation. Thus, the distribution of annual earnings shows more inequality and less positive skewness than the distribution of weekly, hourly, or full-time earnings (Mincer, 1957).[7]

7.3   FEMALE[8] AND FAMILY DISTRIBUTIONS

The relative contribution of employment dispersion to earnings inequality is fairly important in population groups with full and permanent labor force attachment, but it is much more important in

---

7. For an analysis of the effects of cyclical changes in employment on the distribution of earnings see Chiswick and Mincer (1972).

8. For a more intensive human capital analysis of earnings of women, see Mincer and Polachek (1974).

TABLE 7.3
EARNINGS PROFILES OF WOMEN AND MEN, BY SCHOOLING, 1959

	Years of Schooling [a]							
	Elementary		High School		College		All	
Age	Women	Men	Women	Men	Women	Men	Women	Men
Hourly Wage Rates								
25–34	1.37	2.18	1.78	2.57	2.55	3.30	1.82	2.62
45–54	1.43	2.54	1.83	3.16	3.01	5.33	1.85	3.18
All	1.41	2.40	1.74	2.78	2.77	4.31	1.76	2.87
Coefficients of Variation of Annual Earnings								
30–34								
All workers	.62	.47	.60	.50	.56	.51	.69	.57
Year-round	.41	.42	.38	.46	.41	.48	.49	.52
50–54								
All workers	.65	.52	.62	.64	.56	.67	.68	.73
Year-round	.47	.47	.48	.59	.50	.65	.55	.67
30–54								
All workers	.69	.67	.70	.66	.62	.68	.77	.74
Year-round	.49	.59	.48	.58	.50	.62	.57	.67

SOURCE: Hourly wage rates: Fuchs (1967, Table A-1); coefficients: 1/1,000 sample of U.S. Census, 1960.

a. In upper panel, "elementary" refers to individuals with 5–8 years of schooling; "college," to those with 16 years or more. In lower panel, "elementary" refers to 8 years of schooling; "college," to 16 years. "High school" refers to 12 years of schooling in both panels.

groups whose attachment is weak. Men and women exemplify these differences in labor force behavior. The distribution of annual earnings of men is largely similar to the distribution of full-time male earnings. However, the earnings distribution of all women workers is quite different from the full-time distribution. The inequality in annual earnings of all women workers is larger than the inequality in the comparable male distribution, while the opposite is true of full-time earnings (Table 7.3).

Some of the differences between earnings distributions of men and women can be explained by the effects of labor supply behavior on human capital investment decisions. Individuals who expect to spend only a part of their adult lives in the labor force have weaker incentives to invest in forms of human capital which primarily enhance market productivities than persons who expect to be permanently attached to the labor force. Women are likely to invest less than men in vocational aspects of education, particularly in on-the-job training. This is reflected in the comparative (to males) structure of their *full-time earnings* by flatter age-earnings profiles (Table 7.3, upper panel), smaller variances within school and age classes, and less aggregate inequality of earnings (Table 7.3, lower panel).

The changes of relative inequality with age and schooling that we observed in the earnings structure of men are also less pronounced in the full-time earnings of women, and completely obscured in annual earnings (Table 7.3, lower panel).

Mean annual earnings of women are substantially lower than earnings of men. Sex differences in employment behavior and in human capital investment behavior are important causes of differences in means, as they are in affecting the variances and shapes of each of the distributions. An intensive analysis of these differences is outside the scope of the present study, as are comparisons of white, nonfarm men with other groups of men.

Given the greater variance and lower mean of earnings of female workers, a distribution of earnings of all workers, which includes both sexes, must show a greater inequality than the earnings of men alone,[9] as is clear from the aggregation formula (2.12):

$$\sigma_T^2 = \frac{1}{n} \Sigma n_i (\sigma_i^2 + d_i^2).$$

From many points of view, the "intensive" aggregation of male and female earnings within family units is of greater interest than the "extensive" aggregation of persons. Certainly, analyses of consumption behavior and notions of economic welfare are more closely linked to family than to personal distributions of income.

For simplicity, let us abstract from nonemployment income. Then, as a matter of arithmetic, dollar dispersion in family earnings is a positive function of the variances in earnings of family earners and of the correlation between these earnings:

$$\sigma^2(Y_T) = \sigma^2(Y_M) + \sigma^2(Y_F) + 2 \text{ Cov } (Y_M, Y_F); \qquad (7.4)$$

where $Y_M = L_M W_M$; $Y_F = L_F W_F$. Here T denotes family; M, husband; F, wife; L, hours of work; and W, wage rate. The sign of the covariance

9. This is confirmed by the data shown in Schultz (1971, Table 2).

depends partly on the correlation between the earning power (wage rates) of family members, and partly on their labor supply functions. The correlation between earning power, which is positive (classified by education for example), tends to impart a positive sign to the covariance; however, the income effect in the labor supply relations tends to influence the covariance in the opposite direction.

It is perhaps easiest to explain these tendencies if we consider the sign of Cov ($\ln Y_M$, $\ln Y_F$) which, on the assumption of monotonicity, is the same as the sign of Cov (Y_M, Y_F):

Let the labor supply function be:

$$\ln L_F = \alpha + \beta \ln Y_M + \gamma \ln W_F. \tag{7.5}$$

By (7.5):

$$\ln Y_F = \alpha + \beta \ln Y_M + (1 + \gamma) \ln W_F. \tag{7.6}$$

If $\ln Y_F$ is regressed on $\ln Y_M$, the observed slope is:

$$\beta' = \beta + (1 + \gamma)b_{W_F Y_M}, \tag{7.7}$$

where $b_{W_F Y_M}$ is the slope of the regression of wives' wage rates on husbands' earnings, in logs.

$$\beta' \gtreqless 0 \text{ as } b_{W_F Y_M} \gtreqless \frac{\beta}{1 + \gamma}. \tag{7.8}$$

Empirical work on labor supply functions (cf. Mincer, 1962; Cain, 1965; Bowen and Finegan, 1969) of married women suggests that β' is close to zero; hence Cov ($\ln Y_M$, $\ln Y_F$) is in the neighborhood of zero. Since $b_{W_F Y_M}$ is smaller when Y_M contains more of the transitory components, the covariance tends to a smaller positive or larger negative size in such groups.

When relative variances are considered, it is convenient to use the expression:

$$Y_T = Y_M(1 + R_F), \tag{7.9}$$

where $R_F = Y_F/Y_M$. The covariance $\ln Y_M$, $\ln (1 + R_F)$ is of the same sign as

$$\text{Cov} (\ln Y_M, \ln R_F) = \text{Cov} (\ln Y_M, \ln Y_F - \ln Y_M) \tag{7.10}$$

$$= \text{Cov} (\ln Y_M, \ln Y_F) - \sigma^2(\ln Y_M).$$

Clearly if the first term on the right in equation (7.10) is close to zero, as seems to be the case, the covariance on the left must be large and negative. Again, it is stronger when Y_M contains transitory elements than otherwise.

The conclusion that the correlation of components of family income, Cov (Y_M, Y_F), is likely to be small, and even smaller when the earnings of heads of household contain transitory elements, implies that *dollar variances* of family earnings exceed those of husbands' earnings, and more so in families where husbands work full time.

Similarly, the conclusion that Cov (ln Y_M, ln R_F) is large and negative suggests that *relative variances* of family income tend to be smaller than the inequality of the separate earnings of husbands or of wives, though this is less likely in distributions restricted to full-time working husbands.

These implications are empirically verified in Table 7.4 (page 126, below) based on the 1/1,000 sample of 1959 Census data, as they were previously in the 1950 BLS Survey of Consumer Expenditures.[10] Growth of the female labor force, while increasing the earnings inequality among all persons, has actually been a factor in the mild reduction of money income inequality among families.[11]

7.4   AGGREGATION OF OMITTED GROUPS

The population group of white, nonfarm men, the major empirical focus of this study, represented about 70 per cent of all male earners in 1959. Omitted are all nonwhite men, as well as white men who are students, men over 65, farm workers, and the self-employed. These omitted groups of male whites are characterized by highly dispersed, fluctuating, and often intermittent earnings. Analysis of their earnings distributions is outside the scope of this study. This is not to say that human capital analysis is not applicable to these groups. It is true, however, that employment variation, which is treated in a largely ad hoc manner in this study, must receive a great deal of attention in the analysis of such groups.

As far as overall inequality (measured in variances of logs) is concerned, the addition of a comparable nonwhite group to the white group (nonstudent, nonfarm, less than 65 years of age) in-

---

10. Cf. Mincer (1960, Table 4). Both tables show family incomes rather than earnings, a source of rather slight inaccuracy.

11. Cf. findings of D. Metcalf (1971) for the United States, and of H. Lydall (1959) for Britain.

TABLE 7.4
HUSBANDS' EARNINGS (Y_H) AND FAMILY INCOME (Y_T), 1959

	$\overline{Y}_H$	$\overline{Y}_T$	$\sigma(Y_H)$	$\sigma(Y_T)$	$\sigma(\ln Y_H)$	$\sigma(\ln Y_T)$
All Families, Wife Present						
Age						
15–24	3,560	5,180	2,080	3,310	0.695	.616
25–34	5,510	6,830	2,850	3,780	0.557	.511
35–44	6,610	8,454	4,210	5,520	0.586	.547
45–54	6,520	9,100	5,100	6,520	0.656	.612
55–64	5,970	8,620	5,200	6,790	0.754	.683
65 and over	4,310	7,140	5,430	6,690	1.046	.750
Schooling						
5–8	4,690	6,610	3,040	4,230	0.697	.610
12	6,060	7,960	3,790	5,070	0.678	.600
16	9,000	11,210	6,950	8,450	0.678	.600
All	5,890	7,530	4,330	5,580	0.692	.628
Husbands Working Year-round						
Age						
15–24	4,070	5,530	2,070	3,290	0.527	.518
25–34	5,880	7,140	2,840	3,770	0.453	.451
35–44	7,040	8,880	4,250	5,650	0.488	.490
45–54	7,110	9,710	5,340	6,720	0.534	.538
55–64	6,660	9,310	5,490	7,030	0.612	.610
65 and over	6,140	8,980	6,390	7,740	0.782	.639
Schooling						
5–8	5,300	7,180	3,120	4,280	0.497	.508
12	6,370	8,220	3,790	5,100	0.476	.483
16	9,550	11,750	7,060	8,660	0.593	.575
All	6,490	8,460	4,460	5,800	0.540	.536

SOURCE: 1/1,000 sample of U.S. Census, 1960.

creases inequality by no more than 2 percentage points. This is because the nonwhite group is relatively small, and its relative variance is not larger than that of the white group. The small effect is due almost entirely to the differences in means of the two groups.

When all male wage and salary earners are compared with the more homogeneous subgroup we studied, the (log) variance of annual earnings rises to 0.78 from 0.67. Finally, inclusion of self-employed and nonemployment income raises aggregate inequality in male annual earnings to 0.92.[12]

It is worth noting, though without elaboration at this point, that whether we move toward a more inclusive ("extensive") aggregation of population groups, as described here, or an "intensive" aggregation of income into a larger recipient unit, as described in the comparison of husbands' and family income, the characteristic age-schooling structure of income which we observed in earnings of white men remains very similar. Thus, the empirical "predictions" of human capital analysis are not fatally obscured by differences in concepts of population, recipient unit, or even (to some extent) income.[13]

---

12. This is probably an understatement, as nonemployment income is underestimated in the Census.

13. This despite the different effects on inequality that are produced by "extensive" and "intensive" aggregation. My examples of each suggest that extensive aggregation tends to widen inequality (relative dispersion), while intensive aggregation tends to narrow it. A more rigorous statement is that an extensive aggregation of components produces an aggregate relative dispersion which *exceeds* the weighted average of component dispersions, while intensive aggregation produces a smaller than average inequality. The tendency to widen inequality by extensive aggregation is simply due to the existence of differences among means of components $d_i^2 > 0$, in aggregation formula (6.5). The opposite tendency in intensive aggregation is best viewed in terms of the coefficient of variation: given components of earnings, Y_c with mean $\bar{Y}$ and variance σ_c^2, mean of total earnings $\bar{Y}_T = \Sigma_c \bar{Y}_c$, and $\sigma(Y_T) = \sigma(\Sigma_c Y_c) \leqslant \Sigma_c \sigma_c$. Only if the components are pairwise positively and perfectly correlated is the standard deviation of a sum equal to the sum of standard deviations. Hence the aggregate coefficient of variation

$$CV_T = \frac{\sigma(Y_T)}{\bar{Y}_T} < \frac{\sum_c \sigma_c}{\sum_c Y_c} = \sum_c \frac{\bar{Y}_c}{\bar{Y}_T} \, CV_c.$$

In the special case, where all CV_c are the same, aggregate inequality CV_T is necessarily less than the component inequality CV_c.

8

Summary and Agenda

8.1 SUMMARY OF FINDINGS

The first task of the study was to derive and estimate the relation between accumulated investments in human capital of workers and their earnings. This human capital earnings function was then applied to answer two questions: (1) How much of the existing inequality in the distribution of labor incomes can be attributed to individual differences in investments in human capital? (2) Can the intricate yet rather stable patterns of the earnings structure be understood in terms of human capital investment behavior? The "earnings structure" is the aggregate earnings distribution and its partition into schooling and age subgroups. The "patterns" are the comparative sets of means, variances, and shapes of the component and aggregate distributions of earnings.

The summary which follows is by no means comprehensive, nor does the exposition follow the sequence or methods of the analysis. The findings are described broadly and somewhat selectively in terms of the three research objectives of the study:

8.1.1 THE EARNINGS FUNCTION

If completion of schooling meant completion of investment in human capital, the earnings function would be approximately estimated by a simple regression of earnings (in logs) on years of schooling. As the present study indicates, the observed correlation using this "schooling model" is rather weak. Variation in earnings associated with age is not captured by the schooling model, and this omission is, in part, responsible for the low correlation. Though age can be viewed as an inherent depreciation phenomenon in the human capital terminology, the growth of earnings with age can ultimately be interpreted in the human capital model as being a consequence of net self-investment activities that are continued after the completion of schooling. The theory predicts that investments are concentrated at younger ages, but continue at a diminishing rate throughout much of the working life; because of increasing marginal costs, investments are not made all at once in a short period, but are staggered over time, and decline continuously, both because benefits decline as the payoff period shortens, and because opportunity costs are likely to rise with experience. This is true of both gross and net investments.

Since earnings are a return on cumulated net investments, they also rise at a diminishing rate over the working life, and decline when net investment becomes negative, as in old age. The typical (logarithmic) working-life earnings profile is, therefore, concave from below, as illustrated in Chart 4.3. Its rate of growth is a positive function of the amount invested and of the rate of return. Its degree of concavity depends on how rapidly investments decline over time. In effect, the earnings profile is directly proportional to the cumulated investment profile. The magnitude of the cumulated investment cannot to be observed, but it is a concave function of experience. Hence, to expand the schooling model into a more complete earnings function, the linear schooling term must be augmented by a nonlinear, concave, years-of-experience term. This function can be applied in multiple regression analysis to earnings data of individuals who differ in both schooling and age. While age is not the same as work experience, the latter can be estimated as actual age minus estimated age at completion of schooling, though direct information on experience is preferable. Clearly, direct information on experience is necessary for specifying earnings functions of individuals whose attachment to the labor force is not continuous.[1]

The human capital earnings function may be expressed either in dollars or in logs. In part, the choice depends on whether absolute or relative earnings inequalities are to be examined. If dollar values are used, the investment variables (schooling and experience) must also be expressed in dollars. If log earnings are used, then the investment variables can be expressed in units of time—years of schooling and years of experience. The time measures of investment are far more readily available than the dollar ones. For both reasons then—interest in relative comparisons and data availability—the logarithmic formulation is preferred.

The next choice concerns the specification of post-school investment as a function of time. Here the only guidance provided by theory is that annual instalments of post-school investment, and, a fortiori, their time-equivalents, must decline over the working life.

The form of the investment profile determines the form of the earnings profile. To take the two simplest forms, a linear investment decline implies a parabolic experience function, while an exponential decline of investment ratios gives rise to a type of Gompertz function. The latter yields a somewhat better fit, though such discrimination is rather weak. The Gompertz curve requires no decline of the earnings profile, a condition that is largely satisfied if data are restricted to four decades of working life and to weekly (or hourly) earnings. These conditions are fulfilled in the empirical analyses of annual earnings when weeks worked during the year are used as a standardizing variable.

The two forms of the human capital earnings function used in the analysis are the logarithmic parabola (P) and the Gompertz curve (G):

$$\ln E_{s,t} = \ln E_0 + r_s s + r_p k_0 t - \frac{r_p k_0}{2T} t^2; \tag{P}$$

$$\ln E_{s,t} = \ln E_0 + r_s s + \frac{r_p k_0}{\beta} (1 - e^{\beta t}). \tag{G}$$

$E_{s,t}$ is gross annual earnings of a worker with s years of schooling and t years of work experience. "Gross" earnings are inclusive,

---

1. Analyses of female earnings demonstrate dramatically that it is experience rather than age that matters (Mincer and Polachek, 1974).

"net" earnings exclusive, of investment expenditures. r_s and r_p are rates of return on schooling and post-school investments, respectively. k_0 is the ratio of investment to gross earnings at the start of work experience, and β is the annual decline of this ratio. T is the positive net investment period.

In principle, the earnings function represents a unification of analyses of investment parameters and income distribution; it provides an analytical expression for the earnings profile as an individual growth curve. Its coefficients combine estimates of rates of return and volumes of investment. At the same time, the coefficient of determination of the multiple regression measures the fraction of total earnings inequality (variance of logs) that can be attributed to the measured distribution of investments in human capital.

The standard procedure for estimating a rate of return to education involves discounting of differences in earnings between two groups differing in education. However, the estimated rate is not a rate of return to schooling but a weighted average of returns to schooling and to other investments in human capital in which the two groups differ.

In contrast, the earnings function regression procedure does not require pairwise comparisons and can be used to separate estimates of rates of return to schooling from the rates on other (post-school) investment activities. In the empirical work, the estimates of rates of return to schooling are produced unambiguously, but this is not quite true of the rate on post-school investments. Rough tests of the difference between these parameters are possible, however: at the present aggregative level of information, the null hypothesis of no difference cannot be rejected. Whether rates of return differ at different schooling levels can also be tested. The finding is that rates decline as schooling level rises for annual earnings, but not for hourly or weekly earnings.

Use of earnings functions also makes it possible to study the relation between schooling and post-school investments. In dollar volumes the relation is found to be positive. This finding is consistent with a notion of complementarity between the two investment forms, but does not constitute a proof. The positive correlation may simply mean that in comparing individual lifetime investment programs, the scale of investments varies more than their composition. On the basis of the comparative advantages enjoyed by different people and differing relative price structures among them, individuals substitute one form of investment for the other. Yet, because of similar ability and opportunity constraints in schooling and in job training, individuals tend to invest more or less in both. Evidently, scale effects outweigh substitution effects.

It should be noted that though more educated people invest more dollars after completion of schooling, they do not spend more time in post-school investments. The investment-earnings ratio would measure the amount of time (in years) spent in investment (training) activity, if only expenditures of time were involved. On the average, the correlation between "time-equivalents" (that is, investment-earnings ratios) of school and post-school investments appears to be weakly negative. The opportunity cost of an hour is, of course, greater at higher levels of schooling; hence, there is a positive correlation between dollar volumes of investment and schooling, even though "time" volumes are uncorrelated.

The Gompertz curve is a familiar empirical representation of industrial growth. Its fit as an individual growth curve of earnings is no mere coincidence, as the staggered investment interpretation is suitable in both cases. There is a widespread view that differs with this interpretation of individual earnings growth. According to this view, the individual earnings curve is intrinsically an age phenomenon: it reflects productivity changes due to inherent biological and psychological maturation, leveling off early and declining much later because of declining physical and intellectual vigor. There is evidence, however, to indicate that aging affects earnings only to a minor degree. In data where age and work experience can be statistically separated, the position and shape of earnings curves is found to be mainly a function of experience, not of age. Earnings profiles differ by occupation, sex, and color in systematic ways that cannot be attributed to aging phenomena. What is sometimes thought to be an alternative interpretation of the earnings profiles as "learning curves" is not at all inconsistent with the human capital investment interpretation, provided it is agreed that learning in the labor market is not costless: even if apparently costless differential "learning-by-doing" opportunities exist among jobs, competition tends to equalize the net returns, thereby imposing opportunity costs on such learning.

8.1.2 Accounting for Income Inequality

As noted before, if only years of schooling are used in the earnings function, the correlation between years of schooling and (log) earnings of men of working age is less than 10 per cent. This does not mean, however, that schooling is unimportant. In part, the correlation is low because a mere counting of school years does not adequately measure direct costs of schooling and related quality aspects of education. Moreover, when the effects of post-school investments are not explicitly specified, they obscure the effects of schooling on earnings. If post-school investments differ among individuals and are important, the distribution of earnings will be increasingly affected by returns to accumulating post-school investments as years of experience increase. If post-school investments are not strongly correlated with schooling, the correlation between schooling and earnings will continuously decay with the passage of years of experience. The correlation between time-equivalents of school and post-school investment is certainly weak. The correlation between earnings (in logs) and schooling (in years) is, indeed, initially strong, reaching a coefficient of determination of one-third before the first decade of experience is over, but it declines continuously thereafter.

Theoretically, the correlation would be highest at the outset of work experience if post-school investment costs were included as part of income. Such initial "gross" earnings cannot be observed. However, the distribution of observed ("net") earnings 6–9 years later is likely to resemble the distribution of initial "gross" earnings, since net earnings are less than gross earnings, and both rise as post-school investments cumulate; after some years, net earnings begin to exceed the level of initial gross earnings. This "overtaking point" is reached after at most $1/r$ years of experience, where r is the rate of return to post-school investments. Hence this point is reached before the first decade of experience is over. In this period we observe the highest correlation between earnings and schooling.

The coefficient of determination (.33) of schooling and earnings within the overtaking subset of the earnings distribution represents an estimate of the fraction of earnings inequality that can be attributed to differences in years of schooling, since earnings are then least affected by post-school investments. The inequality of earnings at overtaking is about 75 per cent of aggregate inequality, which suggests that the distribution of schooling accounts for 25 per cent of the total (.33 × .75). Together, 50 per cent of aggregate inequality, measured by the variance of logs of annual earnings, can be attributed to the distributions of schooling and post-school investments (Chapter 3). The 50 per cent figure is an understatement, however, since actual rather than time-equivalent years of schooling were used. These fail to reflect quality differences among schools or the variation in expenditures of time and money among students attending schools of the same quality. An upward correction of the variance of schooling investments to take account of such individual differences would raise the explanatory power of schooling to about one-third of the aggregate, and the joint effects of school and post-school investments to about 60 per cent. Transitory variation in weeks worked during the year accounts for another part of aggregate earnings inequality. If so, perhaps as much as two-thirds of the inequality of "normal" (longer-run) earnings can be ascribed to the effects of the distribution of education and experience.

The estimates quoted above are largely indirect inferences, described in Chapter 3. If we restrict ourselves to direct (and incomplete) regression estimates, we find that even with the use of only two variables—years of schooling and of experience—the explanatory power of the earnings function regressions compares favorably with results of statistical studies of comparable microdata which employ a large number of explanatory variables on a more or less ad hoc basis.[2] It is far superior when weeks worked during the year is added as an explanatory variable.

It appears that the substantive conclusions about the quantitative and qualitative importance of human capital investments in the distribution of earnings are not much affected when the population is extended from white urban men to all men in 1959, or changed from (male) persons to family units.

8.1.3 THE EARNINGS STRUCTURE

There are several prominent features of the "skill" (schooling and experience) structure of earnings which appear rather stable in tem-

---

2. For a review of some of these studies, see Jencks et al. (1972).

poral and regional comparisons. Aggregate skewness and the growth of inequality with age are the best known. To these there may be added patterns of dispersion (variances) cross-classified by schooling and age. These are less familiar and perhaps also less stable.

The characteristic features of earnings distributions, such as aggregate skewness, and the relation of inequality to skill (or schooling) and age (or experience) have puzzled observers since detailed statistical data became available. Partial explanations, largely of the "random shock" variety, have been proposed.

In the human capital model, most features can be explained by the correlation between the stock of human capital at any stage in the life cycle and the volume of subsequent investment. That this correlation is positive in dollar terms is understandable, if individual differences in ability and opportunity which affect investment behavior tend to persist over much of the life cycle. The positive correlation between schooling and post-school investment is an example of such persistence in behavior. (See Chapters 2 and 6.)

Several implications of the positive correlation between successive instalments of investment in human capital in dollar terms can be observed: Dollar profiles of earnings "fan out" with experience and, a fortiori, with age, both across and within schooling groups. Dollar variances in these groups, therefore, increase with experience and with age. Similarly, because the dispersion of dollar schooling costs increases with the level of schooling, variances of earnings increase with level of schooling. Since mean earnings increase with age and with schooling there is a positive correlation between means and variances in age and schooling subgroups of the earnings distribution. This correlation contributes to the appearance of positive skewness in the aggregate earnings distribution. This factor is independent of, and in a way more basic than, the shape of the distribution of schooling, which in the past also contributed to the positive skewness of earnings. The change in the distribution of schooling during the past two decades from positive to negative skewness implies that the distribution of schooling is no longer an important factor in explaining the persistence of positive skewness in the distribution of earnings. Indeed, the 1959 distribution of earnings at the overtaking stage of the life cycle is not skewed at all. The aggregate distribution, however, remains positively skewed.

If we define relative skill differentials in wages by percentage differentials in wage rates among schooling groups having comparable years of *experience,* we find that these are almost invariant over the working life. Since the logarithmic experience profiles of wages are concave, this finding implies that relative wage differentials among schooling groups increase with *age.* However, *within* schooling groups, relative wage dispersions, measured by variances of logs, show somewhat different profiles, depending on the level of schooling. When plotted against age, all are U-shaped along at least some portion of the curve, and clearly so at the center of the schooling distribution, that is, for the high-school group (see Chart 6.2). For the post-high-school group, the profile is mainly increasing. Within lower schooling groups, it first decreases and then levels off.

It was shown that both the wage differentials between schooling levels and the inequality patterns within the middle levels of schooling reflect a negligible correlation between post-school earning capacity and time-equivalent post-school investment. This same lack of correlation underlies the previously noted invariance between experience and relative wage differentials among schooling groups. The phenomenon arises if experience profiles of post-school investments, in time-equivalent units, are not systematically different among schooling groups. Put another way, it arises when the elasticity of post-school investments (in dollars) with respect to post-school earning capacity is, on average, unitary across schooling groups. Within schooling groups, however, the elasticity of investment with respect to earning capacity appears to increase with schooling level: it is less than 1 at lower levels and greater than 1 at higher levels.

The size of the elasticities and the systematic positive relation between schooling level and elasticity of investment with respect to earning capacity raise questions for further research. In this connection, it is noteworthy and suggestive that very similar patterns are found in studying the consumption function: The "long-run" elasticity of saving with respect to income is not clearly different from 1, and the "short-run" or cross-sectional elasticity increases with schooling level (Solmon, 1972).

The differential patterns of log variances by schooling level can also be analyzed by age: the ranking of log variances of earnings is inverse to schooling level at young ages, positive at older ages. Also, the age-schooling profiles of absolute and relative wage distributions aggregate to the well-known leptokurtic shape, with a skewness that is positive in dollars and negative in logarithms. Together with some observations on correlations of earnings of members of a Consumers Union panel, the distinctive profiles of relative variances constitute strong evidence for the human capital and against the purely stochastic theories of income distribution: Systematic, rather than chance, variation dominates individual earnings histories and individual differences in earnings.

8.2   SOME QUESTIONS AND AN AGENDA FOR FURTHER RESEARCH

8.2.1   ABILITY, OPPORTUNITY, AND INVESTMENT

The model of worker self-investment as the basic determinant of earnings might be criticized as giving undue weight to the supply of human capital while ignoring the demand side of the market. Certainly, demand conditions in general, and employer investments in human capital of workers in particular, affect wage rates and time spent in employment, and thereby affect earnings. It should be clear, however, that the earnings function in this study is a "reduced form" equation, in which both demand conditions and supply responses determine the levels of investment in human capital, rates of return, and time worked. The present approach is an initial and simple one, and greater methodological sophistication is clearly desirable. There is a need to relate employers' behavior both as demanders of and direct investors in human capital to the observed distribution of earnings.[3]

The investment-earnings relation in this study is in reduced form also in the sense of describing equilibrium loci in the (human) capital market as well as in the labor market in which human capital is supplied as a factor of production. As Becker describes in his analysis, the cross-sectional earnings function results from two simultaneous structural relations in the (human) capital market. These are demand functions (D_i), which relate individual investments to marginal rates of return, and supply functions (S_i), which relate the volume of funds that can be obtained for human capital investment to their marginal "interest" costs. Of course, worker demand for self-investment (D_i) is, in part, derived from employer demand for the workers' human capital.

---

3. For an interesting attempt in an analysis of the earnings distribution in Japan, see Kuratani (1972).

The amount the individual invests, the magnitude of his marginal and average returns, and therefore the volume of his earnings are simultaneously and optimally determined by the intersection of the demand and supply curves. Overall labor and capital market conditions determine the group (or sectoral) levels of the D and S curves, individual levels of demand are determined by tastes and abilities, and differences in levels of supply curves represent differences in investment financing opportunities. Thus, it is equally correct to say that the distribution of earnings is determined by the distribution of accumulated human capital and of rates of return to human capital investment or that the distribution of earnings is determined by the distribution of ability and opportunity. Or, putting it in a causal hierarchy, the distribution of accumulated human capital is a proximate determinant of the distribution of earnings, and is treated that way in this study. In turn, ability and opportunity determine the distribution of human capital, and this is the focus of Becker's (1967) analysis.

A low correlation between investment in human capital and earnings would not constitute a rejection of the human capital hypothesis. Of course, if we had information on both volumes of investment and rates of return for each worker, the relations would be perfect and tautological. However, we are relating only volumes of (accumulated) investment to earnings, while the variation in rates of return and in unmeasured quantities of investment are left in the statistical residual. Thus, aside from such measurement error, the correlation reflects the structure of individual supply (opportunity) and demand (ability) conditions in the cross section: the wider the dispersion of supply and demand intersections (i.e., of rates of return at given volumes of investment), the weaker the correlation. The correlation would be perfect if any of the following were true: perfect equality of opportunity (i.e., a common supply curve for all); perfect equality of ability (i.e., a common demand curve); or perfect positive correlation between ability and opportunity. The greater the departure from these conditions, the lower the correlation.

The fact that rates of return are negatively or not at all related to schooling level suggests that inequality of opportunity (dispersion of supply curves) is at least as great as inequality of ability (dispersion of demand curves). At the same time, the positive association of indexes of ability (I.Q. and other test scores) to investments (schooling) suggests that ability and opportunity are positively associated among individuals. Indeed, with sizable inequalities in ability and opportunity from individual to individual, the correlation of human capital with earnings would be weak unless the correlation between individual ability and opportunity were quite strong.

A single cross section, such as the 1959 one in this study, does not yield much insight into these aspects of the social structure, but can provide a frame of reference for studying changes by means of repeated analyses of comparable periodic data, such as decennial censuses.

To the extent that ability and opportunity affect rates of return but not volumes of investment, they create residual variation in earnings at given levels of human capital. The earnings function could be expanded to incorporate ability or opportunity variables to account for some of the residual variation.[4] However, the question in this study is not what explains earnings, but what are the effects of human capital investment on earnings. Moreover, the residual contains unmeasured components of investment, such as quality of schooling and within-group variation in post-school investment. Even in the residual, therefore, ability and opportunity may be acting on earnings via investment, rather than independently.

It is widely believed that the omission of ability from the earnings function creates a specification bias: leaving out a variable which is positively correlated with earnings and investment biases the coefficient of investment (average rate of return) upward. Whether this argument is correct depends on the concept of ability and the causal structure of the model: if ability affects earnings *only because* it affects investment in human capital, one of the variables is redundant when both are entered in the earnings function.[5] When the

---

4. Note, incidentally, that at fixed levels of investment, ability and opportunity are perfectly negatively correlated. Both, therefore, could not be entered as explanatory variables in the same equation.

5. A similar redundancy occurs when parental education is entered in the earnings function. Parents' education is positively correlated with the education of their children. Unless parents' education has an effect on children's earnings aside from affecting the investment in their human capital, its inclusion will obscure the estimated effects of human capital on earnings.

Another redundancy may result from the inclusion of occupation together with education in the earnings function. Occupational advancement is a medium by which growth in human capital leads to higher earnings power. Entering both variables as coordinate leads to an apparent and misleading reduction in the coefficient (rate of return) of education.

variables are not coordinate, but hierarchical, they should be treated recursively.

However, a specification problem does arise in my formulation of the earnings function. The function specifies accumulated (invested) human capital, while observed earnings are a return on the total human capital stock, including "original" or "initial" components and those not accumulated in the forms explicitly specified in the function, yet correlated with them. "Ability" may be viewed as such an "initial" component, or E_0 in my earnings function. Empirical measures of ability, as imprecise as they are, have been found to be positively associated with both schooling and earnings. Empirical estimates of the bias in the rate of return (coefficient of the schooling variable) due to the omission of ability average less than two percentage points, as against an uncorrected estimate of the rate of return which exceeds 10 per cent.[6] If these findings can be taken at face value, I have overstated the explanatory power of *accumulated* human capital to some extent.

8.2.2 FAMILY INVESTMENT IN HUMAN CAPITAL OF CHILDREN

The process of investment in human capital is not restricted to schooling and job training. Much of it takes place in the home, particularly during the preschool stage of the life cycle, as well as later. In empirical studies of intergenerational influences on educational attainments it has been found that the education of parents is a significant variable. This may be interpreted as evidence either of the transmission of parental tastes and motivations or of the greater propensity of more educated parents to invest in the education of their children, or both. One form of this investment is more and better schooling. Another is the time and other resources parents spend on their children, which we may call "home" investments. These investments were not specified in my earnings function. Although time devoted to children may be viewed as a parental consumption activity, to the extent that measurable opportunity costs

---

6. This conclusion was reached in Becker's preliminary investigation (1964), and has not been modified by a series of more intensive recent studies. See Griliches and Mason (1972), Hause (1972), and a survey by Welch (1972). Somewhat greater bias was found in a sample studied by Taubman and Wales (1972).

are involved, an investment model can be developed for research purposes and can be used in the earnings function framework.

The visibility of these opportunity costs emerges from research on labor supply, viz., women reduce their market work to take care of their young (particularly preschool) children. The reduction in earnings which results from the reduction of time spent in the labor market is a direct measure of the opportunity cost of these investments. Estimates of these costs are feasible.[7] Their analysis should contribute to the explanation of phenomena such as the importance of family background in school performance of children; the effects of growing up in a broken home; the positive correlation between educational attainment of children and that of their parents, particularly that of the mother. Whether and how much these preschool investments affect the children's earnings beyond affecting school attainment of the child can only be answered by the proper incorporation of the variable in the human capital earnings function.

The promise of this kind of research is its contribution not only to an understanding of the observed distribution of income at a point in time, but also to the analysis of intergenerational social and income mobility. Inferences about mobility depend on the strength of the correlations between family income and education of parents, as well as on the structure of parental labor supply functions at different levels of education and income. Depending on such parameters, the same earnings function can produce different mixtures of perpetuation and reshuffling of poverty and affluence.

8.2.3 THE DISTRIBUTION OF EMPLOYMENT AS A COMPONENT OF THE EARNINGS DISTRIBUTION

Annual earnings are a product of the wage rate and of time spent in gainful employment. Thus the distribution of employment is an important component in the distribution of earnings, all the more so as the correlation between wage rates and employment appears to be positive, at least in the 1960 data: more skilled workers have higher annual earnings both because they are paid more per hour, and because they work more during the year.

---

7. Research into these matters is currently being conducted by Arleen Leibowitz at NBER. See Leibowitz (1972). See also Mincer and Polachek (1974).

Much of the individual variation in weeks and hours of work is random, particularly over short periods such as a year. Nevertheless, some of the employment variation may be attributed to differences in human capital, that is, to skill and experience differences among workers. The differences in employment, which consist of differences in labor force participation and in unemployment, originate both on the demand and supply side of the market. A number of hypotheses involving labor supply functions, health differentials, employer demand and investment in workers, household and market production functions,[8] and institutional factors, such as minimum wages and income maintenance programs, can be brought to bear on the analyses of the employment distributions. Once the relation between employment and wage rates is better understood, the employment variable, which is simply entered multiplicatively (additively in logs) in the earnings function, will be more appropriately specified. The expanded earnings function will appear as a product of two functions: the wage rate, or productivity, and the employment function, with independent variables in each. This is a schematic and operational representation of how the labor market interacts with households to produce the observed distribution of earnings.

8.2.4 FURTHER ELABORATION OF EARNINGS FUNCTIONS

The earnings function in this study represents an initial attempt at a more comprehensive formulation than the rudimentary schooling model. The next development would be a more detailed specification of various forms of human capital and of investment activities, beyond the general categories of schooling and post-school investment. Parental investments in children, particularly preschoolers, were already mentioned. Among other aspects of initial capacity, health levels should also be included. Both investments in health and the life cycle of human capital depreciation, including the important problems of obsolescence, deserve special attention.[9]

The specification of schooling investments in this study leaves out direct cost components and students' earnings. As was indi-

---

8. These are the subject of current research at NBER. See Mincer (1973).
9. For a beginning on the subject of health in the context of human capital, see Grossman (1972 and 1973). For attempts at analysis of depreciation plus obsolescence, see Koeune (1972) and Rosen (1974).

cated, such data, when available, can be entered in the earnings function quite easily.[10]

Perhaps the most important and urgent task is to refine the specification of the post-school investment category. First, direct information is needed on years of experience. In the present study years were estimated as age minus (estimated) year of graduation. For persons fully and continuously attached to the labor force this proxy variable may serve well enough. (Still, even the analysis of male earnings would be improved by direct information on experience, as the National Science Foundation studies suggest.) For persons whose labor force attachment is partial and discontinuous such information is indispensable.[11] Of course, we need to remember that it is not the time spent in the labor market, but the volume of investment activity taking place during that time which determines earnings. Comprehensive data on this do not exist, but intensive even if fragmentary case studies might be feasible.

Even when work experience is measured in time units, the total of it could be segmented into a sequence of jobs constituting the work history of the individual, if data were available. Whether in chronological or, preferably, in panel form, this is ultimately the way in which the analysis of labor mobility should be incorporated into the human capital framework.[12] Search for and the acquisition of job information are topics pertinent to the subject of labor mobility, but their inclusion in the earnings function would depend on the availability of data meeting rather exacting specifications.

8.2.5 TOWARD A FULLER ANALYSIS OF INCOME DISTRIBUTION

In sum, fuller analysis of the distribution of earnings would require both an expansion of the earnings function to include details (variables) on a number of forms of investment in human capital, as well as a system of equations that includes not only the investment-earnings relation but a formulation in which investment is the de-

---

10. Some work along these lines is currently being done by Solmon and Wachtel (1972) at NBER.

11. This point emerges forcefully from papers by Malkiel (1971) and Polachek (1973) and Mincer and Polachek (1974).

12. Longitudinal data recently collected in the National Longitudinal Samples and by NBER (NBER-TH sample) make possible a start on such analyses.

pendent variable and another in which (time spent in) employment is the dependent variable.

Coverage of the data used for the analyses should be expanded to include women, blacks, older people, and people who live in nonurban areas. Moreover, grouping of persons into households as well as their behavior as members of households, needs to be studied in the context of income distribution. For this, the merging of population, labor supply, and human capital theories is required.

Finally, to move toward the distribution of income as distinguished from the distribution of earnings, nonemployment income must be brought into the analysis. This is not merely an accounting problem. Attention will have to be extended from human capital to the interaction of human and nonhuman capital accumulation and use by households, and to the effects of transfer incomes on both.

Bibliography

Adams, F. G. "The Size of Individual Incomes: Socio-Economic Variables and Chance Variation." *Review of Economic Statistics,* November 1958.

Aitchison, J., and Brown, J. A. C. *The Lognormal Distribution.* England: Cambridge University Press, 1957.

Bates, W. D. "A Formula for Finding the Skewness of the Combination of Two or More Samples." *Journal of the American Statistical Association,* March 1935.

Becker, G. S. *Human Capital.* New York: NBER, 1964.

———. "Human Capital and the Personal Distribution of Income." *W. S. Woytinsky Lecture No. 1.* Ann Arbor: University of Michigan, 1967.

Becker, G. S., and Chiswick, B. R. "Education and the Distribution of Earnings." *American Economic Review,* May 1966.

Becker, G. S., and Ghez, G. "The Allocation of Time and Goods Over the Life Cycle." Processed. New York: NBER, 1972.

Ben-Porath, Y. "The Production of Human Capital and the Life-Cycle of Earnings." *Journal of Political Economy,* August 1967.

———. "The Production of Human Capital Over Time." In *Education, Income and Human Capital.* Studies in Income and Wealth 35. New York: NBER, 1970.

Birren, J. E. "Psychological Aspects of Aging." In *International Encyclopedia of the Social Sciences,* Vol. 1, 1968.

Bjerke, K. "Income and Wage Distributions." Processed. Copenhagen: May 1969.

Blum, Z. D. "Income Changes During the First Ten Years of Occupational Experience." Report No. 122, Center for Social Organization of Schools. Baltimore: Johns Hopkins University Press, 1972.

Bowen, W., and Finegan, T. *The Economics of Labor Force Participation.* Princeton, N.J.: Princeton University Press, 1969.

Box, G., and Cox, D. "An Analysis of Transformations." *Journal of the Royal Statistical Society,* Series B, 1964.

Cain, G. G. *Married Women in the Labor Force.* Chicago: University of Chicago Press, 1966.

Chiswick, B. R. "Human Capital and Personal Income Distribution by Region." Ph.D. dissertation. Columbia University, 1967.

———. "Income Inequality: Regional Analyses Within a Human Capital Framework." Work in progress. New York: NBER, 1973.

Chiswick, B. R., and Mincer, J. "Time-Series Changes in Personal Income Inequality." *Journal of Political Economy,* May 1972.

Craig, C. C. "On the Frequency Function of XY." *Annals of Mathematical Statistics,* March 1936.

Folger, J. K., and Nam, C. B. *Education of the American Population.* Census Monograph, 1967.

Friedman, M. *A Theory of the Consumption Function.* Princeton, N.J.: Princeton University Press, 1957.

Fuchs, V. R. *Differentials in Hourly Earnings by Region and City Size.* Occasional Paper 101. New York: NBER, 1967.

———. "Differences in Hourly Earnings Between Men and Women." *Monthly Labor Review,* May 1971.

Goodman, L. "On the Exact Variance of Products." *Journal of the American Statistical Association,* December 1960.

Griliches, Z., and Mason, W. "Education, Income and Ability." *Journal of Political Economy,* May 1972.

Grossman, M. *The Demand for Health.* Occasional Paper No. 119. New York: NBER, 1972.

Hanoch, G. "An Economic Analysis of Earnings and Schooling." *Journal of Human Resources,* Summer, 1967.

Hansen, W. L. "Total and Private Rates of Return to Investment in Schooling." *Journal of Political Economy,* April 1963.

Hause, J. C. "Earnings Profile: Ability and Schooling." *Journal of Political Economy,* May/June 1972, Part 2.

Heckman, J., and Polachek, S. "The Functional Form of the Income-Schooling Relationship." Processed. New York: NBER, 1972.

Hill, T. P. "An Analysis of the Distribution of Wages and Salaries in Great Britain." *Econometrica,* 1959.

Jencks, C., et al. *Inequality.* New York: Basic Books, 1972.

Johnson, T. "Returns from Investment in Schooling and On-the-Job Training." Ph.D. dissertation. North Carolina State University at Raleigh, 1969.

Juster, F. T. *Anticipations and Purchases.* New York: NBER, 1964.

Juster, F. T., ed. *Education, Income, and Human Behavior.* Carnegie Commission on Higher Education. New York: McGraw-Hill, 1974.

Koeune, J. C. "The Obsolescence of Human Capital." Ph.D. dissertation. Columbia University, 1972.

Kuratani, M. "Specific Training and Income Distribution in Japan." Ph.D. dissertation. Columbia University, 1973.

Leibowitz, A. "Education and Allocation of Women's Time." Processed. New York: NBER, 1972.

Lydall, H. "The Long Term Trend in the Size Distribution of Income." *Journal of The Royal Statistical Society,* Series A, Part I, 1959.

———. *The Structure of Earnings.* New York: Oxford University Press, 1968.

Malkiel, J., and Malkiel, B. "Sex Differentials in Earnings." Processed. Princeton University, 1971.

Metcalf, D. "Income Distribution in the Business Cycle." *American Economic Review, Papers and Proceedings,* May 1971.

Miller, H. P. Census Bureau Technical Paper No. 8, 1963.

———. "Education and Lifetime Income." *Current Population Survey,* 1967.

Mincer, J. "A Study of Personal Income Distribution." Ph.D. dissertation. Columbia University, 1957.

———. "Investments in Human Capital and Personal Income Distribution." *Journal of Political Economy,* August 1958.

———. "Labor Supply, Family Income and Consumption." *American Economic Review,* May 1960.

———. "Labor Force Participation of Married Women." In *Aspects of Labor Economics.* Universities–National Bureau Conference 14. Princeton, N.J.: Princeton for NBER, 1962 (1962a).

———. "On-the-Job Training: Costs, Returns and Some Implications." *Journal of Political Economy,* Supplement, October 1962 (1962b).

———. "The Distribution of Labor Incomes: A Survey." *Journal of Economic Literature,* March 1970.

———. "Education, Experience and the Distribution of Employment and Income. In Juster, ed. (1973).

Mincer, J., and Polachek, S. "Family Investments in Human Capital: Earnings of Women." *Journal of Political Economy,* March 1974.

Morgan, J., et al. *Income and Welfare in the United States.* New York: McGraw-Hill, 1962.

———. "The Anatomy of Income Distribution." *Review of Economic Statistics,* August 1962.

Polachek, S. "Post-School Investments and Sex Differentials in Earnings." Ph.D. dissertation. Columbia University, 1973.

Reder, M. "A Partial Survey of the Theory of Income Size Distribution." In *Six Papers on the Size Distribution of Income and Wealth.* Studies in Income and Wealth 33. New York: NBER, 1969.

Rosen, S. "Measuring the Obsolescence of Knowledge." In Juster, ed. (1974).

Rutherford, R. S. G. "Income Distributions: A New Model." *Econometrica,* July 1955.

Schultz, T. P., "Long Term Change in Personal Income Distributions," AEA meetings, December 1971.

Solmon, L. "Education and Saving." In progress. New York: NBER.

———. "The Relationship Between Schooling and Savings Behavior: An Example of the Indirect Effects of Education." Processed. New York: NBER, 1972.

Solmon, L., and Wachtel, P. "Effects of Schooling Quality on Earnings." Processed. New York: NBER, 1972.

Stigler, G. "Information in Labor Markets." *Journal of Political Economy,* October 1962.

————. *Capital and Rates of Return in Manufacturing Industries.* New York: NBER, 1963.

Taubman, P., and Wales, T. *Mental Ability and Higher Educational Attainment in the Twentieth Century.* New York: NBER, 1972.

Thurow, L. *Poverty and Discrimination.* Washington, D.C.: The Brookings Institution, 1969.

Tolles, N. A., et al. "The Structure of Economists' Employment and Salaries, 1964." *American Economic Review, Supplement,* December 1965.

Tolles, N. A., and Melichar, E. "Studies of the Structure of Economists' Salaries and Income." *American Economic Review, Supplement,* December 1968.

U.S. Bureau of the Census. *Current Population Reports,* Consumer Income, P-60, No. 56, August 1968.

U.S. Department of Labor, Bureau of Labor Statistics. *Seniority in Promotions and Transfer Provisions.* Bulletin 1425. March 1970.

U.S. Department of Labor, Bureau of Labor Statistics. *Educational Attainment of Workers.* Special Labor Force Report No. 83. March 1970.

Weiss, Y. "Investment in Graduate Education." *American Economic Review,* December 1971.

Welch, F. "Black-White Differences in Returns to Schooling." In "Research into Poverty Labor Markets." Processed. New York: NBER, 1972.

Index

GLASSBORO STATE COLLEGE